LIGHT
BRIGHT
DAMN NEAR
WHITE

STORIES AND REFLECTIONS OF
A MULTI-RACIAL BLACK MAN'S
BATTLES WITH RACISM IN AMERICA

RICHARD LAWRENCE

ONEEARTH PUBLISHING

The collage of Lawrence family photos on the cover was created by Clifford Lawrence in 1981. Raymond, child number fourteen, was born with Downs Syndrome and lived for only five years. The picture of him in his walker is the only known photograph.

THIS BOOK IS DEDICATED TO:

THE LAWRENCES

Hazel Kelly Reams/Weems, whose birth certificate is still a mystery, and Benjamin Levi Lawrence, a black Nova Scotian, who together produced fifteen little Lawrences: Emma Leigh, Raymond, Donnie, Freddie, Cynthia, Dickie, Dolly, Cliffie, Virginia, Mabel, Robbie, Charlie, Joey, Benny, George. Their hearts, hands and heads molded me into a proud Lawrence, a feisty black American and an aspiring writer.

MY OFFSPRING

Tony, Valory, B.J., and Abi; and grandchildren Anthony, Bella and Richie Lawrence have loved me and held onto me even after a terribly painful separation and divorce. They are all beautiful, generous and creative free spirits and a tribute to their parents and the human race.

THE TYNINGS of ANDOVER, MA

Especially Nancy, who welcomed me into her heart. Her family helped turn around some bad feelings about Andover and Punchard (now Andover) High School where I could never get a date or even get a girl to dance with me in high school. I graduated from Punchard with honors but never a single word of encouragement to go on to college.

KEN AND BRENDA VAUGHN

and Kenny, Malik and Kilam, who have loved me and shared their home in Chicago with me and taught me priceless lessons, including the beauty of being Black, through classes in their School of Human Dignity.

CORY BRIGGS AND SEEKEY

who reminded me that the Courts are still a good place for fighting for justice and introduced me to tough love for the environment and Open Government.

TONY PERRINO AND MARY ELLEN

who made me a special part of their ministry in BallardVale and pushed me on to Albion College and the Methodist ministry.

SAMANTHA QUIROZ

and her parents, Pedro and Theresa, who have encouraged me from the beginning to write this book and who continue to show me they know how to fight a good fight as partners in Creed 21 and San Diegans for Open Government.

**LEE VAN HAM, FIELDING MCGEHEE
AND VICTOR BLOOMBERG**

whose faithful friendships, creativity and conversations pulled me out of the many wormholes I managed to find and fall into on my way to publication.

CUMMINS ENGINE FOUNDATION

and Irwin Miller, Ambassador Jim Joseph and Lt. Gov. Phil Sorensen who designed a radical innovation in philanthropy and offered me and four other outside agitators the best job any of us would ever have. They inspired an understanding that charity is only a first step toward justice, and an empty one, unless accompanied by personal engagement in the causes we support.

THE METHODIST CHURCH'S BISHOPS
who made my life miserable and taught me that there
are no perfect institutions, but Methodist preachers—
especially John Porter, Ray Balcomb, Bob Peters, Bob
Burtner, Gerald Forshey and Martin Deppe – all fighters for justice who fought for and won my right to full
ordination and made social justice a real ministry.

REV. DR. MARTIN LUTHER KING, JR.
who called us to march in Selma in 1965 and in Chicago in 1966, and who inspired me to be a man of courage, compassion and commitment. He exemplified a
ministry of social justice and shared his beautiful and
powerful spirit by giving me and thousands of others
a chance to work with him in the Chicago Freedom
Movement alongside Jesse Jackson/ Operation Breadbasket, James Orange, Jim Bevel, C.T. Vivian, Al Raby,
Andy Young and dozens of other Chicago Freedom
Fighters.

WITH SPECIAL THANKS TO...

My sister, **Dr. Cynthia Rose Lawrence,** who introduced me to the adult learning community in Berkeley, CA known as the Western Institute for Social Research (WISR) and its President, John Bilorusky. WISR is a multicultural institution where individual instruction and action research around social change are taken to new heights.

I am proud to share the proceeds from the sales of this book with WISR.

You can learn lots more at www.WISR.edu.

CONTENTS

A NEW BEGINNING

Bedtime finally arrived, but the light bulb directly over my bed made it nearly impossible to sleep. So, I rolled up the newspaper I had found, and with great effort, stretching and strain, I finally unscrewed the bulb. It went out, and I went to sleep.

At roll call the next morning, the officer in charge directed us to form a single line, hollered each of our names and demanded we respond with our name and the word "present" and nothing else. He then read the work assignments for the day followed by a list of those individuals who were to stay in place in their cells. My name was on that list.

I tried to remain calm and waited to find out what was going on. Why was the guard calling my name? Why pull me out of the morning line-up? Did someone come to bail me out? This guy didn't look particularly threatening, but I was warned that I did not want to find myself alone in Cook County Jail with one of the guards. Stories were everywhere that the guards were a more serious threat than the other inmates--although nobody thought the inmates were a joke either.

After everybody else was gone to their work assignments, I didn't dare sit down and thought it might be a good idea not to move. The guard didn't say anything to me for what seemed like a really long time. He continued to shuffle papers until I couldn't stand it any longer.

"Officer. Did you want me to stay?" It sounded like a really dumb question but it was the best I could do.

"Did I call your name?"

"Yes, you did, but I've been standing here for a long time and..."

"You think you've been standing here for a long time? Well, I've got news for you. Your time is my time. You're not going anywhere, mister, until I'm good and ready to take you to solitary."

Holy shit! He said solitary, didn't he?

I immediately apologize to any fellow clergy who might have overheard my unexpected expletive.

"I'm going to solitary?" I asked. "Why? I didn't do anything,"—again feeling just a little stupid.

"Oh you didn't?"

I tried hard to think. What could he be talking about?

"You think you can make your own rules, do ya? You think you don't have to do what everybody else in here has to do and can turn out the lights when you feel like it?"

Another officer—a sergeant, I think—finally arrived.

"Well, Mr. Lawrence, you need to take off your clothes," were the sergeant's first words, and a chill went through me as I wondered again if the rumors about guards that folks insisted on sharing with me were true.

I stared at the man.

"Take off all your clothes and put them in this bag—and your shoes too."

"I don't understand."

"You do speak English, don't you?"

"Yes, I do."

"Then take off your clothes. You're already in trouble, so I'd suggest you don't make things any worse. "

"How can I be in trouble? I haven't done anything."

"Oh? You haven't done anything? You broke a house rule. You clearly have a problem respecting our rules…and we're not very fond around here of agitators who disrespect cops either, so you're going to spend some time in solitary until you get it right."

Comforted somewhat by the dimming likelihood that I was about to be raped, I tried to picture exactly what it was I had done and how I was supposed to know the "house rules" since this was my first night in the Chicago House of Corrections—a place with a reputation of not being as bad as the Cook County Jail, but not that much better either.

"Officer, I still don't understand."

"Well then let me explain something to you. That night light over your bunk is for your protection, and when you turn it out, we have to believe either you have a date and want some privacy, or you're sending a general invitation for any inmate who feels so inclined to join you in bed. Turning off that light is a serious violation."

"But I had no idea..."

"Yeah, sure you didn't. A pretty boy like you didn't get those lips from sucking on lemons. You're going to solitary just as soon as the officer finishes his paperwork and can get the relief squad up here to get your clothes and move you out. I can't leave here, but you're goin' one way or another, so just stand there and shut up."

I stood, and I shut up.

In about an hour or so another officer arrived, and he walked me in my underwear through a maze of cells, locked gates and dark hallways.

I was startled when one inmate roared out, "Hey Bro!"

I did not look up. "You don't have to look at me, but I'll remember you. Anybody can see you're light, you can't be too bright, but you damn sure ain't white.

Come on down some time and see what my black ass can do for you."

Reaching solitary confinement was a relief until they took my underwear, gave me a pullover cotton shirt that barely reached my knees and pushed me into a small cell where there was a bed frame and springs but no blankets nor barely any light.

I was in a daze, so I sat on the iron frame of the bed and found myself wondering how in the world I got into this mess. The cop they were talking about my harassing was Burleigh Ginkle. I had tried to have a prayer with him at his home after everything else we tried failed to get a hearing for Richard Hagan, a former Golden Gloves boxing champion and sparring partner of Joe Louis. Hagan was stopped on a traffic violation and shot dead by Officer Ginkle, a resident of Gage Park, the community where Dr. King and those of us marching with him had been stoned during one of our Open Housing Marches. Hagan was shot and killed in front of his six year-old son. The officer thought the boxer was reaching for a weapon, but no weapon was found. The Chicago Police did not even so much as call for an internal investigation, and the black community was furious. So, we marched some more—this time to Officer Ginkle's home where James Orange, a staffer with King's SCLC, and I were arrested. I would not pay the $100 fine on the principle that an injustice had been ignored and paying the fine felt like an announcement to the world that it was OK with me. It was not.

I had been assured by my lawyer that I would not spend any time in jail because the statute under which I was being held had been declared null and void by the Illinois Supreme Court. But as I feared, that did not make any difference to the judge in my case. The Chicago "Democratic" machine of Richard J. Daley got judges elected, so I was sentenced to jail even in the face of an appeal to Justice Thurgood Marshall of the U.S. Supreme Court on the fundamentals of habeas corpus, no body (of law) existed to support the arrest.

The whole mess I was in was a painful reminder of why I never intended to spend any time in jail;, but in the late spring of 1965, the students at Wilson Junior College (now Kennedy-King Community College) and Chicago Teachers College (Chicago State University) were determined that something had to be done about race relations in Chicago. They were still angry that we had failed to save the job of a Parker High School teacher fired for teaching Black History. Parker High shared a campus with Chicago Teachers College and once was the student teacher placement preference for most teaching candidates until the high school student population turned all black.

Our students heard about other college students from across the country making history as leaders of the freedom movement and leaders of the sit-ins and the freedom rides. The Student Non-Violent Coordinating Committee (SNCC—pronounced "SNICK") was now deep into recruiting college students to join the effort to register black voters all over the South, and we heard from a number of them.

We couldn't help but notice that while buses were burned and riders were beaten on the freedom rides and sit-ins, there was something intensely different about the violence around voter registration. All of us had heard of Goodman, Cheney and Schwerner and their work in Philadelphia—not the home of the Liberty Bell—but the home to members of the KKK in Mississippi where those three young students "disappeared" and died trying to register voters there.

News stories were everywhere about the latest violence in the police blockade on the bridge in Selma, Alabama, where hundreds of freedom marchers headed for Montgomery were trampled by troopers on horseback, choked by tear gas and clubbed by other troopers running after and brutally beating any retreating marcher they could catch. Bloodied marchers lay on the ground everywhere, and March 7, 1965, became known across the country as "Bloody Sunday".

So, our students rallied on campus in support of the Freedom Fighters. We had videos and speeches that highlighted the awful truth about Selma where whites were ready to do anything to be certain that no more black voters were allowed to register. It was simple math: Blacks outnumbered whites in Selma, but not one black held an elective office, and Selma wanted to keep it that way.

The speaker from SNCC the organization that was sponsoring "Freedom Summer", the voter registration campaign in which Goodman, Cheney and Schwerner participated, really laid it on:

"Alabama is one crazy place," he hollered, and then he paused. "Dr. King has joined SNCC in calling for help from preachers, students and other folks from all across the country to come to Selma and join in another march for freedom. It is no picnic. We just learned that Rev. Jim Reeb, a Unitarian minister from Boston, was beaten on the street in Selma today and is in a hospital—but NOT IN SELMA, because they refused to treat him there. He is in critical condition in a Montgomery hospital, and the word is he may not make it."

"Sheriff Clark in Selma said to the press that it was not his job to protect 'outsiders who come to Alabama to make trouble', so if you're going to Selma, you are on your own."

The students insisted: "WE ARE GOING TO SELMA", and so my VW bus was packed with canned goods, covered with a mattress, and five students and I—black, white, male, female—were on our way to answer the call to join the fight for freedom.

SELMA

From Selma, Alabama, the call went out across the nation for preachers, teachers and everybody else who wanted to be freedom fighters, especially volunteers from the North. We were all asked to collect money and send or bring food and clothes to support the Freedom Marchers in their struggle to register the black voters of Alabama's Dallas County.

John Lewis, now a US Congressman, and hundreds of other marchers had been trampled and beaten by Alabama State Police at the foot of the Edmund Pettus Bridge on "Bloody Sunday", March 7, 1965. Police, some on horseback, were determined to stop the marchers from reaching Montgomery, the state capital, where they hoped to present their case to the governor and the nation. Qualified blacks were illegally and violently being denied their right to register and vote. To augment the marchers, rallies and teach-ins were organized across the country in support of the call to Selma.

Our rally on the campus of Chicago Teachers College was designed to encourage students to learn about Selma. Learning about the history, out of which the violence in Selma was born, turned out to be an enormous success, and the Campus Christian Association for which I served as campus minister, collected several hundred dollars and about a ton of food to support the Selma non-violent fighters for justice.

The students argued that it was time to do more than that and wanted to join the fight for voting rights on the real battlefield. They were not to be denied, so we began to plan for the trip to go into the deep, rural South for the first time and join marchers from all across the country.

The Voter Rights Movement was committed after "Bloody Sunday" to make yet another march over the Edmund Pettus Bridge. The march would involve folks from all over the nation and would cover all 45 miles ending in a huge voter registration rally in Montgomery and bring what Dr. King called "the white heat of truth" to bear on Selma, an example of a national disgrace that denied blacks the vote.

It is tough to believe today that all this was required, and it is equally incredible that blacks in the South could not vote in 1965—more than 100 years after Emancipation. "Any means necessary"—a phrase later to become popular in the work of the black Panther Party—was employed by Dallas County officials who were determined to stop voter registration campaigns by "outside agitators".

Violence and physical intimidation during the Bloody Sunday march and confrontation at the bridge in Selma reached unprecedented levels. Less violent, but more widespread and subtle efforts across the South included ad hoc tests employed to disqualify black voters—tests that no whites registering to vote were required to take. It was virtually impossible for most blacks to pass such tests, and college students recruited from across the country by SNCC were now engaged in trying to teach black voters a new kind of academic art—cramming for the County Board of Election Registrar's literacy tests.

The march from Selma to Montgomery, the state capital, hoped to call attention to the fact that the governor and other state officials permitted and encouraged such injustice and steadfastly refused to do anything about it. Federal action was needed. There were calls for a Constitutional Amendment to guarantee every citizen the right to vote. Short of that, federal registration of voters and federal marshals were needed to oversee the local registration process and to protect blacks who were courageous enough to attempt to register. If blacks could register and vote, it was obvious that the South would change, and change was not what the white minority wanted to see.

Our job on the march, and the job of other Northern supporters, Hollywood personalities and big names, was to build up the morale of the local residents and to provide them physical protection by our presence in a march that required the President to federalize the National Guard and send in hundreds of federal marshals.

Once we decided we had to go, the students and I removed the seats from my VW bus and loaded boxes of canned food on the floor. We covered those cans with a mattress and had one big bed so all of us could share the driving and sleep while taking turns at the wheel.

Five students and I made the trip—black and white, male and female. As we entered Kentucky—the first "Southern" state on our journey—a shiver went through us all. We were in the South, and fears about going even deeper into the South than any of us had ever traveled before were nearly palpable.

As our fear deepened, our laughing and singing grew louder and bolder. We really did not know what to expect, and we did not want to think about what we knew of the South—of lynchings, of Chicagoan Emmett Till's death because he smiled at a white woman, of burning crosses and white-hooded terrorists. Nothing could distract us, and every eye of every rider in our van was trained on the landscape hoping to identify any threat before it became a deadly reality.

The reality that we saw was a cloud of blue smoke trailing behind us as we were driving along. Not long after the first sighting of the blue smoke, our engine failed altogether. When I opened the engine compartment, I knew we had serious engine trouble. Motor oil was everywhere.

We were about 10 miles outside Louisville, and we all held our breath as the wrecker hauled us to our first encounter with somebody from "the real south". The VW dealer's service manager examined our vehicle. We discussed what we would do if he charged us an unbearable amount for the repairs or if he refused to fix our VW bus at all. We decided we would sit-in right there at his dealership and call our friend at the *Chicago Sun-Times*, who had seen us off and done a story on our trip. To our surprise, the service manager ushered us into the waiting room and offered us all coffee in a manner true to the best traditions of southern hospitality.

The only bad news was that our enthusiasm had outweighed our good sense, and our VW had been asked to convey a heavier load than its engine could handle. We had blown it, and we had to lighten our load and replace the engine.

We decided to call the Selma March office. We were told that if we could reach a local number right away, the food in our VW could be transferred to a truck bringing supplies being shipped that day from local churches in Louisville. "You mean to tell me there are people in Louisville sending food and supplies to Selma?" I inquired. "There sure are," said the southern voice at the other end of the line with a clear laugh at my question.

After the call, our discussion shifted to whether we could pay for the engine repairs with the money we had collected for the Selma March. We decided that we could, and were back on the road in a matter of several hours after the dealer agreed to store the heavy boxes of food until the truck arrived to pick them up.

We were learning a lot about the South. But as the darkness approached, our fears leaped back at us as we drove through the night and entered Alabama. Every one of us was awake and alert—watching for and occasionally seeing eyes of evildoers in the woods and shadowy movements behind which we feared might be a loaded gun. We all admitted it: we were alone on a dark Alabama highway, and we were terrified. This was no fun at all. Where were the marchers and the folk singers and movie stars and the other supporters when we needed them most?

We decided to sing at the top of our lungs: "Woke up this morning with my mind...set on freedom. Woke up this morning with my mind set on freedom. Woke up this morning with my mind set on freedom. Allelu..., Allelu...,Allelu-u-u-u-jah."

"Driving and singing with my mind set on freedom..."

After we had exhausted our knowledge of freedom songs, we sang love songs and folk songs and children's songs and hymns from church and silly songs and only on rare occasion did someone break the magic of the music with the sudden, "What was that?".

The intensity of the sudden fright turned our stomachs sour, and we had to swallow several times to be sure everything would stay in place. Finally, we reached Brown Chapel in Selma, and there was a rally scheduled for later that night. To our disappointment, Dr. Martin Luther King Jr. was nowhere to be found.

In the meantime, we were all given several hours of nonviolent training by someone we had never heard of and told what we could expect and were made to practice how to accept the jeers and taunts of folks who would attack us with stones and sticks and words as we marched.

And then we were asked to volunteer for one of the work teams for the march: food and site preparation, security, marshals, etc. Two of us chose site preparation and were disappointed to learn later that we could not march with the main march but would have to drive ahead of the marchers to clear the pastures and set up the tents where the marchers would eat and sleep over the four days of the full 45-mile trek.

We complained so much it was finally agreed we would all start out on the March and would then fall out and be driven to our assignment. Those campsites were home to hundreds of cows who dumped thin, brown pillows on the ground regularly and generously. None of us wanted to sleep in or on them, so we had to scoop up every one, bag them and stack them for removal. On our site preparation crew was actor Gary Merrill, who worked beside us like any normal human being would and avoided the news media, which attracted other stars like Harry Bellefonte, Joan Baez, Pete Seeger, Paul Newman and dozens of others I saw and forgot. I did not forget Mr. Merrill.

Each night on the March, there was a show which these and other performers presented to the marchers to cheer us up and help us forget about our tired feet or aching backs. We finally heard Dr. King with hundreds of thousands of others when we arrived in Montgomery at the voter registration rally. We were so far back in the crowd that we could not see him, but the PA system allowed us to hear the eloquence and fire which made it all worthwhile and inspired us to even greater determination to help set things right in any way we could.

All of us were to meet back in Selma for the trip home to Chicago, and about half of our original group had arranged a ride back to Selma with me in our VW van which had reclaimed from its noble service as a march vehicle. By the time we found each other, it was getting dark in Montgomery and rumors were flying that the Klan was out looking for marchers. We were told to head directly to Selma on the prescribed route and not to stop for anyone we didn't know. It was ecstasy and agony. Being present for such an event was wonderful and inspiring, but the night once again presented the menacing threats with which we had become so familiar—shadows of red-necked locals who had shouted and cursed us all along the route of the march and crackling sounds that we were sure was gunfire that only our newly learned discipline kept us from ducking.

Suddenly, a flashing set of red lights appeared behind us, and a fearful silence replaced the excitement and stories of the day. I did not want to stop, but it was clearly an official Alabama state trooper, so I decided we had no choice. Our uncertainties about what to expect did not exempt Alabama state troopers, and I thought of my torture and death in the woods after the troopers turned me over to the local Klansman. I wondered if I would be brave or cowardly in the face of my torture and death. I asked the students to be quiet. We had agreed earlier that we would not be led off like sheep, like the victims of the gas chambers. We would run into the Alabama night in as many different directions as possible making it impossible for the officers to catch us all.

With that reminder about our agreement, I stopped the VW van and waited. One officer remained in the cruiser. The other approached and asked, "Did you folks see a dark blue or black Chevy about 1957-58 coming at you from the opposite direction?" My voice was lost in a mass of mucus clogging my throat, and I was barely able to whisper my reply, "No, Sir, officer. I couldn't really see anything. It's dark on this road."

I immediately regretted what sounded slightly like a smart-aleck remark that might be taken as a criticism of things in the wonderful State of Alabama.

The officer did not notice and persisted, "Are you sure you didn't see anything at all of a vehicle matching that description?" I repeated my assurances as best I could being sure not to say anything even vaguely critical of Alabama, and the officer's response surprised me. "You all need to be very careful and be sure you stay on this road. Do not stop for anyone and get right back to Selma as fast as you can." The trooper nearly ran back to his vehicle, flashed his lights at us so we could get back into traffic, and then sped by us on his way to continue his search for this mysterious vehicle.

Our curiosity was doubly piqued. How come this Alabama trooper was so concerned about us and how come he was so nice?

About an hour later we pulled into the church parking lot in Selma to meet the rest of the crew from Chicago, and there was a general buzz. Rumors persisted that someone had been shot on the road from Montgomery to Selma, and we told our story of the encounter with the state trooper which added additional fuel to the rumor fire.

We had to be on our way home so left Selma unsure of what had happened. We were almost in our now "beloved" Kentucky when we heard confirmation on the radio that Viola Liuzzo, a mother from Detroit who was taxiing marchers back to Selma, had been killed by a shot fired from a speeding vehicle being sought by the authorities.

Members of our group began to cry in a mixture of sorrow, fear and joy that we were free from the burden someone else had been called to carry for us. One and all spoke of their vow of never turning back from the call of freedom which woke us, called us, drove us and would use us to help make a new day when there would be fear no more.

Selma is the County Seat of Dallas County, Alabama. In 1961, the population of Dallas County was 57% black, but of the 15,000 blacks old enough to vote, only 130 were registered (fewer than 1%). At that time, more than 80% of Dallas County blacks lived below the poverty line, most of them working as sharecroppers, farm hands, maids, janitors, and day-laborers.

Led by the Boynton family (Amelia, Sam, and son Bruce), Rev. L.L. Anderson, J.L. Chestnut, and Marie Foster, the Dallas County Voters League (DCVL) attempted to register black citizens during the late 1950s and early 1960s. Their efforts were blocked by state and local officials, the White

Citizens' Council, and the Ku Klux Klan. The methods included a literacy test, economic pressure, and violence.

MY MOTHER

My Mother...

She takes me from a warm, warm cot

and puts me on a cold, cold pot and

makes me go whether I gotta or not.

My Mother.

...a poem I learned from my brother, Cliff

My mother, Hazel Kelly Weems Lawrence, bore each of her fifteen children one by one and reared them in an all-white small town in Massachusetts called Ballardvale. Ten boys and five girls grew up at my mother's knee, plus an uncounted number of adopted children and pets she took in from time to time. "There's always room for one more," she would say. Her most famous addition to the family may have been a cat that looked so bad when she brought him home we named him "Sad Sack," a name so fitting he was tagged for life.

As if rearing those fifteen children was not enough, my mother worked doing laundry, sewing, ironing and taking care of other families' children. We needed the money.

After 40 years of marriage, however, she had the older boys pile their father's belongings in the driveway and kicked him out of the house because she had had enough of his violent, drunken outbursts. She put it simply, "Pa didn't hold up his end."

All of us were responsible for "holding up our end" and doing anything that needed to be done around the house. Ma would call out: "Dickie, Dollie, Cynthia, Cliffie, Robbie...whoever you are...get in here." We all learned to cook and clean and iron and sew—skills that served us well.

When we went to work as kids picking strawberries or doing other summer jobs, we were expected to contribute half of what we earned "to support the house." It was not debatable nor do I recall any of us arguing about it.

If one of us needed to be disciplined, Ma would send the villain out to the yard to cut a switch which she would use to give a licking. She always swatted around the waist and below. If we thought we could lighten the punishment by bringing back a brittle branch that easily broke, she would break it on us and then send us back for another and take up where she left off.

Of our fifteen, there were, as you would expect, some problems. My brother, Raymond, the fourteenth of fifteen, was born with Down's syndrome—but back then, everyone called him a "mongoloid". My mother refused to have him institutionalized until the very end, although everybody told her she should. She ignored the practice of the day and kept Raymond at home and cared for him. She badly underestimated the challenge of providing the needed care, and her devotion took a significant toll on her health.

While still caring for Raymond, my mother became pregnant with child number fifteen and had to ship her other younger children out to stay with friends. Some of us have very unpleasant memories of that time, but I am fortunate to have no memory of that at all. My sister, Cynthia, thinks that's because I probably wasn't shipped out because "Dickie was always Ma's favorite."

My mother was sure to send us to Sunday school somewhere—Baptist, Congregational or Methodist—so it is no surprise that I have a special place in my heart for Sunday school and this poem of Alice Walker's:

"Who made you?" was always
The question
The answer was always
"God."
Well, there we stood
Three feet high
Heads bowed

Leaning into
Bosoms.
Now
I no longer recall
The Catechism
Or brood on the Genesis
Of life
No.
I ponder the exchange
Itself
And salvage mostly
The leaning.

"Sunday School, Circa 1950,"
Revolutionary Petunias

I have been leaning toward others all my life seeking the warmth of being included, and it is a shock when I think I never leaned against my own mother or father. They did not cuddle me, and so after being away at Albion College in Michigan—then a state I thought was "out west"—I decided that when I got home I was going to hug my mother and tell her that I loved her. I succeeded with the hug, but her apparent uneasiness and impatience with me did not allow me to get the loving words out.

Nonetheless, I never felt neglected. I always knew I was loved, and whatever my mother could not deliver in parental love and support because she was busy with one of the other fifteen of us, my older sisters and brothers made up for. They took good care of us and enjoyed the right to tell us what to do that came with that responsibility and were usually generous with affectionate discipline.

My mother's father, the man I knew as my grandfather, was not my mother's biological father. Grandpa Summers married my grandmother while she was pregnant with another man's child. There is much confusion about this, and my mother grew up thinking her birth name was "Reams." When forced to apply for U.S. citizenship after marrying my father, a man from Nova Scotia, Canada, she discovered there was no Hazel Kelly Reams of record born in Boston on her birthday, April 28, 1901. She "adopted" the name of "Weems," as there was a Hazel Kelly Weems born on that date.

My father, Benjamin Levi Lawrence, came from Nova Scotia, which came to mean for us "a land where men were pig-headed bulls of enormous strength, heavy drinkers and junkmen who kept everything." Benjamin was also a master stone mason who could do just about everything with bricks and mortar and was renowned for the stone walls he built without mortar. He would offer his gigantic dump truck and challenge his customers to drive into the wall with it and try to knock it over.

When it came to collecting payment for his work, however, my father was no master, and it is impossible to explain how my mother and father expected to feed and care for fifteen children. If all of us had been angels and in perfect health, they might have pulled it off.

My keenest recognition of the kind of mother she had been dawned on me when I appeared at Albion College as a freshman with a total of $200 in hand and faced a bill then due and payable for $265. I did not panic, and Albion College created what I believe was its first work-study program enabling me to enroll and clean classrooms to make up the money needed to stay in school.

Our family was poor, but it took several sociology classes for the reality of the poverty we faced to sink in. Even when it did, it did not bother me. I shared my insight with the family, and we used to laugh about always putting the milk bottle on the table—a sure sign we met the academic definition of being lower class.

My mother's gifts and abilities deserve recognition and a super special award. She was not a perfect parent. She did not encourage any of our family members to freely express affection to one another, and most of us found her challenge of advancing the cause of interracial relations seriously inhibited us. She imposed a challenge on each of us that we always be on our best behavior so that we exemplified that "Negroes" were fully human and deserved to be accepted by whites. I took that mandate very seriously and lived an inhibited life, by nearly always carefully monitoring what I was thinking of saying or doing.

This inhibition in no way disrupted my sense of feeling secure and loved, and being a happy kid.

I remember when I was first inspired by the local minister to consider going to college. I knew I was smart and had very good grades, but it seemed natural that I would finish high school and go to work and help support the family until I got married. I was number ten of fifteen children, and the contributions of my older brothers and sisters had made things easier around the house. Though I had never considered college and thought I ought to do my part to help out at home, I broached the subject with my mother.

"Ma, Rev. Perrino thinks I ought to go to college."

"Well...," she paused and looked pleasant—not quite smiling. "What do you think of that?" She was kneading bread with the heels of her hands, and it was not at all clear whether her response was a statement or a question.

"I thought you might need me to help out around the house."

"You could set the table."

"Ma, I set the table last night. It's Cynthia's turn."

"If I could only get you kids to do something without grumbling all the time about whose turn it is."

She reeled off a list of the names of her kids in a loud shout trying to call for Cynthia, but her anger got the best of her memory. "Donny, Freddie, Dolly, Cliffie..." She let the list hang there and threw some more flour on the waxed paper covering the table. She tossed the dough onto the waxed paper.

"When you kids get my goat I can't see straight, and I sure can't remember one of you from the other. When my ship comes in I'm gonna hire a housekeeper and let her keep track of all of you."

Cynthia came dashing into the kitchen, a room that attracted a lot of attention because the wood stove served as the central heating plant for the entire upstairs. Grandpa lived downstairs and owned the place, but for some reason there were no heating vents running to the upstairs from the big coal-burning furnace in the cellar.

"Ma, did you call me?" Cynthia asked expecting a medal for answering the general alarm.

"Yes, I did—about a dozen times."

Cynthia shrank. She wanted to say, "Yes, you called me and half the population of Massachusetts too," but she knew better. That kind of sass would only irritate my mother who would send her out to the backyard to cut a switch for a licking.

"Will you please set the table, Cynthia?"

Ma could go from a hard-nosed commander to a gentle guide in nothing flat.

"You got a college in mind, Dickie?"

"No, but Rev. Perrino thinks it would be good for me to go away to a small college and live in the dormitory. He says that's where the real education is, so he wrote for a couple of catalogues from Methodist colleges in Michigan."

"Michigan? Are you sure you're ready to go out to the Wild West for school?"

The bread was on its way into the oven shining white from the Crisco she had rubbed on it. My mother managed to keep her back to me by fiddling with things on and around the stove.

"Ma, Michigan isn't that far away, and it's not the Wild West."

"Well, I guess we can get along without you around here. You've helped out quite a bit, but we got along before you were old enough to get to work, and we'll get along without you after you quit and go off to school."

She washed and wiped her hands at the kitchen sink. "I don't think we'll be able to help you out much if you run out of money, and that worries me."

She turned to my sister, Cynthia. "Dickie's going to college in Michigan."

"Is that as far as we can send him?" Cynthia bumped her backside into me jolting me out of her way.

"Cynthy, you're just jealous," I said as I backed toward the kitchen door, "'cause you know if we were sending you anywhere it wouldn't be to college. It would be to Danvers State Hospital Mental Ward."

I darted away, but I knew she'd get even somehow. Her favorite revenge was slowing down while washing dishes when I really wanted her to finish so I could wipe them and get out to the playground for the evening baseball game. When I complained to her about her slow pace of putting dishes into the strainer, she displayed her contempt for my wishes with an infuriating "tsk, tsk, tsk" that made my blood boil.

Little did it matter. I was on my way to a new chapter in the life of the Lawrences—the first among us to find his way to college.

ABOUT MY BROTHER FRED

My brother Fred died at an early age because of an outrageous combination of medical malpractice and ignorance about mental illness. We could do nothing about either, and so my mother's story is included here in the hope her closing words will soon come true.

Fred was admitted to the Lawrence General Hospital with pneumonia, but as he improved physically, he became aggressive and was put into restraints. Doctors looked at his chart and saw that he was on Haldol—a drug he was gradually introduced to over several weeks in another hospital. The doctors did not know enough about the drug and returned him to the high dosage with no gradual introduction, and Fred went into a coma.

My sister, Emma Leigh, and I were called in the early a.m. and asked by the staff if they should try to treat the problem, since his temperature had soared to 107 degrees and "if he survived, he would likely be a vegetable." Our reading was: "this is a useless, mentally ill giant of a man of color who scares the daylights out of us, and we think we might be doing the community a favor if we let him die." Our response was to treat him, and we visited an unconscious Fred, talked to him, played music for him, sang to him and helped him recover only to discover later that the diabetes he suffered and the chemicals he was given combined to deliver a deadly dose of gangrene that knocked him out again.

Since Fred was unconscious, we had to decide to allow the doctors to surgically remove his leg in hopes of stopping the spread of the infection. We said yes, take it.

When Fred awoke, he asked me, "What happened to my leg?" "Fred," I began, "we had no choice. Either we let them take your leg or you were going to die." This man, mentally ill and widely feared, who went to sleep with no thought of losing a leg, looked me in the eye and responded, "Okay, Dick."

It was far from okay.

The combination I mentioned above killed him a few months later.

My mother tells Fred's story below in her own unedited words.

◆ ◆ ◆

This is the story of my twelfth child, Frederick.

Fred is now twenty years old. As a little boy at the age of four he had a terrible skin disease. Now that was in the days of the Depression, and I was hard put to feed my brood of fourteen. I know he didn't get all the medical care only all my love and attention. I did take him to our family doctor a few times, but he could not help as this trouble was beyond him. Well, I used all the home remedies on him, but none of them did any good. He suffered dreadfully.

My husband was working odd jobs here in our little town, and one of his friends married a doctor who lived just three houses down the street from us. He became interested in Fred's trouble and came to see him. He asked me if I would let him try and help, and I was more than happy to try anything at this point. So, Dr. Bleicher came by sometimes as often as six times a day with different medicines each time and told me how to use it.

I must tell you about my family so you can get a good picture. I had ten boys, five girls and a husband at this time (he passed away a few years ago). I lived in the same house with my father and mother. My mother was in a wheelchair crippled. She could not do anything for herself. My father was wonderful but helpless, like a child. He tried to help but did not know how. Also I found out my mother was dying of cancer. At this time, I had a boy in my own family who was two years old and was a mongoloid. I was an only child, so I had no one to help me at this trying time.

Well, getting back to Fred. The doctor cured Fred after two years of working with him, but his trouble left him very nervous. He could not stand loud noises. The doctor said the trouble left him with his nerve ends raw. He had to be loved and petted all the time.

For the next two years, I didn't have any more trouble with him but I had my hands full. Of course my mother got worse and so did my fourteenth child. I had to make up my mind and put him the state hospital. I was doing everything for him and didn't have the strength for the rest of my family.

Then God knew I needed a fifteenth child. I could not accept this at first but at last my faith in God helped me and I had a lovely baby girl. My mother became worse and was very hard to take care of. My dad and I did our best. I was expecting the baby in February and my mother died in December. My poor dad was brokenhearted, so was I, but I still had a life to consider. I don't think I mourned as much as he did because I still had the children to take care of.

Things went as they do with our help, trying to feed and clothe my gang took all my strength. When Ray, the sick baby, took sick at the hospital after only being there five days, he died; at the age of five years. I was really broken up over this and had a long terrible breakdown. I got over it.

When Fred was eighteen—this was after the war. I had five sons in the service at one time, all at the front, later another son joined the Navy, I was very proud of this and scared as I worried about them…but thank the Lord, they all came of it safe. My five oldest married in less than two years.

When Fred reached eighteen, he had what I thought was a breakdown, but It was worse than that. The Red Cross in the town of Andover, who had helped me raise the other children, sent me to Salem to a doctor for advice on Fred. I took my oldest daughter, who was always helping me through thick and thin/we always did all the hard jobs together. Well, this doctor said Fred had to be put in a state hospital for the insane. This almost killed me because I knew nothing about these places, only the talk. I had heard/all bad. The one my baby Ray had been in was for children, and

what I had seen in the two times I went to visit
was very clean and nice. The only thing, it was
a long way from home.

Well, my daughter and I left Salem for
Danvers State Hospital. We admitted Fred and
had to leave him there. I felt I had left part of
my heart there. They do not allow you to see
your loved ones for a few days; until the pa-
tient gets adjusted. Well, I saw Fred later. Dr.
Hess, a lovely, understanding, fat, jolly man,
who I can say really loved his patients, all 2,000
of them, was very understaffed. He could not
possibly know what happens to the patients all
the time. Now the hospital is understaffed also,
and not enough help, I have often wondered in
the past five years why the well patients could
not have helped those that are ill. Maybe this
would not work, but as far as I know it has not
been tried.

Fred, at the first time in the hospital under-
went twenty-one shock treatments! There may
have been others, but I was not told. They are
horrible, but even so he was helped to get better and come home, after about five months
of treatment. Well, Fred was not the same boy
now, he always had a chip on his shoulder;
would not keep a job as he said they would not
pay him enough. Now Fred is six feet tall and
weighs 225, more or less, so, when he aroused

people let him alone. If they didn't he would kill them in one of his rages. He was attacked by two or three attendants once in the hospital.

At this time, after he had been home a few weeks, he had to check into the hospital at least once a month for a check-up. He was not ill but had chewed his tongue and Dr. Hess wanted him to have brain wave tests. Fred begged me not to leave him there, but I was only human and trying to go along with the doctors. I was wrong I think. Anyway, he got into trouble and when I went to see him one Sunday with one of my daughters they asked us not to see him as he was not feeling very well. I went home and came back the following Wednesday; I got the same story.

Well, I had had enough and demanded to see Fred. When I got up to J-3 (the worst was there-anyone who breaks a rule or is hard to handle is there...takes a lot of courage to visit there because of the crying and the cursing, shouting and fist fights among the patients...), well, Fred was in what they called the strong room, with two men standing guard...like a jail...I went in with my daughter and Fred's younger brother. You would not have known the poor boy, his eyes were almost shut, black and blue...I was sure his nose was broken... and of course he was like an animal who had been kicked around and did not trust anyone, least of all me. In this ward I have seen, and so have others, straitjackets which are supposed to be outlawed; they still use them...

Well, I cried, and then got angry! I went to Dr. Hess. He didn't believe me so he called the ward. They told him Fred had fallen and he hurt himself. It took me an hour to get the doctor to go see for himself. When he got back he was talking in German and was very cross. Well, we went home angry and called the doctor that had directed us to Danvers. He told us to bring Fred home. (He had been on the staff there, too). Oh, how wrong he was...

As we waited for Fred to come down from the ward we must have had all the doctors warn us not to take Fred home. Now they cannot stop a parent from taking their loved ones out.

Well, we came home and Fred was very ugly all the time on the way home, but I just knew in my heart that he would be alright with all our love...but how wrong I was...at home he was still cross. The next morning I was making cakes for two of my grandchildren and as I was bending over to look at the cakes, Fred took a paring knife and thrust it into my back. It was such a hard blow I almost went into the oven. I did not know I was stabbed. Then Fred would not let his brother, his baby sister and myself come out of the room. He played with us like a cat with a mouse. If I never spend another morning like that, it will be too soon. At last he turned to his brother and said, "Now go call the police, I need a ride back to Danvers." Even though he was ill, he knew he would really hurt someone.

Up to this time. I didn't know I was bleeding all over the floor. The police came and took Fred away. He went without putting up a fight. Then I was told I was stabbed and I went for X-rays...they were afraid my lung had been punctured. After waiting for three hours, and looked at by many doctors, I had three stitches taken in my back.

I was a wreck, heart-sick and weary... BUT...with the faith I have had all my life knowing God does not give His loved ones more than they can bear...I would have given up—in fact I did, but with the love of my family I lived again.

Fred would come home in the spring for the good weather, but every fall he gets sick again...so we go through this year after year, and the doctors give us no hope.

Now the youngest brother, Donald, joined the Navy at age 17. He went to Europe and became ill and was in the hospital in Europe then they flew him back to the states. He was in Philadelphia until he was cured. He had had a breakdown. The same as I had off and on for thirty years...when things got too big I would hide, but it didn't work because God put us on the earth to work for others, and tells you to love your neighbor, whether you it or not...or family or a stranger...so in Jesus I keep trying.

Don has been in Danvers one year. Now he is in Bedford, a V.A. Hospital, and is doing very well and will be out soon.

Now, the mongoloid baby I had, Raymond, has more than prepared me for the tremendous cross I had to bear. I can truly thank God for giving me this baby, and if this gets printed, may my troubles help someone else to have courage...the kind I got from him.

MY HOMETOWN—
BALLARDVALE,
MASSACHUSETTS

Andover…the home of the bean and the cod,
where the Cabots speak only to the Lodges,
and the Lodges speak only to God.

Andover was not the target of that limerick, but it deserves to be. It is home to beans and cod, Cabots and Lodges, Phillips Academy and Ballardvale.

I have always said that I come from Ballardvale, an idyllic spot on the banks of the Shawsheen River in the Merrimack Valley—home to the cities of Lawrence and Lowell—both giants in their day and producers of textiles for uniforms and blankets for our troops in WWI and WWII. It is unfortunate that prosperity for the textile mills depended on war, and when we stopped having really big ones, that industry died, and the region sunk into a depression from which it has not yet fully recovered—even after moving into the South looking for cheaper labor.

It is curious that Ballardvale, an unincorporated section of Andover, appears on maps of Massachusetts. Shawsheen, historically home to the officers and managers of American Woolen Company and also a section of Andover, does not appear on those same maps nor does West Andover, home to Andover's farmers. I think it is because Ballardvale was disowned by the town of Andover. We were home to working families—laborers in the mills that once used the water power from the Shawsheen River to stimulate the development of the industrial areas of Lowell Junction and Ballardvale.

Ballardvale may have been disowned because Ben Jacques, owner of Ben Jacques Coal Company and employer of my grandfather, Benjamin Summers, bought the abandoned one-room school house and sold it to my grandfather. There were no other black families in Ballardvale, and there was no intention that there would ever being any. Working class families were bad enough, but blacks were unheard of.

The story goes that old man Ballard was a believer in liberty, so when he moved his flax mill to the Vale, he had a replica of the Liberty Bell installed in the cupola. The mill was placed on the Shawsheen River to take advantage of a drop in the flow, and the old man built a small dam to enhance the falls. Water powered a large turbine that turned out the power for the machinery that contributed to a boom in what was to become Ballardvale.

Both the bell and the dam contributed greatly to the entertainment of the kids in town. We knew that if we climbed to the cupola and rang the bell the town police would be called. No one was ever caught so far as I know, but on one occasion we swore we heard a shot. Every one of us swore a bullet had whizzed past his ear.

My own memory was that I not only heard the shot, I felt the impact and dreamed of the collection of friends gathered around me praising my courage in the face of death. My courage was clearly aided by that fact that my dream was devoid of any real feeling of pain. Although mortally wounded, I was quite comfortable.

The wounds suffered by having grown up in Ballardvale, however, were far from free of pain. When our next door neighbor's kids and the Lawrence kids had a fight, they would often end it with an angry, "Why don't you go back to Africa where you belong."

I really did my best to please everyone, as my mother had encouraged me to do—not out of passive indifference, but because it was necessary to advance the cause of improved race relations. So, I did not fight. I led an exemplary life and learned to put responsibility ahead of pleasure. I was conscientious in everything and worked harder than other kids in order to ensure no one had any thoughts of my being lazy or inferior in any way.

My hard work paid off with good grades in high school and an occasional maternal tribute from a friend's mother who scolded her own son with: "Why can't you be like Dickie Lawrence?" That tribute backfired on me as my friends decided that if I weren't around there would be no comparisons.

In the social arena, no amount of hard work paid any dividends at all. There was not a single girl who would dance with me at our high school dances. "Nothing personal, Dickie."

Our family learned about economic downturns and depression, and we became very good at living through them.

Jay Leno grew up in Ballardvale on the same street (Clark Road) where our family homestead still stands occupied by my brother Cliff and his family, but Jay will tell you he grew up in Andover. That is perfectly understandable, because you cannot distinguish Ballardvale from the rest of Andover any longer. Our homestead was probably the last in town without indoor plumbing. I can remember the delight in seeing our outhouse come down, but there was no shame attached to it. It was simply genuine delight when my father literally raised the roof in that old schoolhouse and made room for our first commode and bath tub. Saturday night baths in that big, cold, metal tub with water heated on a wood stove were over.

INTEGRATION, BLACK POWER AND BACK

My first date was arranged for me when I was a junior in college. It was a birthday present from Tony Perrino, the minister to college students at Oregon State University in whose home I was living.

My experience with dating is obviously very limited, because somehow every girl I liked and wanted to date knew I was black and that dating me would cause an immediate family crisis or an international incident of enormous proportions. So, whenever I finally found someone who liked me, I held onto her for as long as possible and did not even think about any other woman. Dating more than one woman at a time was simply not an option.

When I returned to Oregon for my first job, I was surprised and delighted to learn that Dianne Dickson was still single. She was working in her family's drugstore in the Montavilla neighborhood of Southeast Portland.

Dianne had caught my eye while we were both at conferences of the Methodist Student Movement at Camp Magruder near Rockaway on the Oregon Coast. She was vivacious, a lot smarter than me and really cute. We both loved camp songs and the adoration of an audience, and we both thought ourselves to be very accomplished song leaders. She added a dynamic, dramatic flair to her presentations that was hard to ignore. She showed an unusually quick wit and creative imagination in the short skits that played so well on the stage at Camp Magruder.

I bumped into her every now and then with hopes of getting her attention during casual volleyball and soccer games on the beach, but I had no reason to think I had penetrated her filter, but I had. Our romance was intense. I do not think she had dated much more than I, and we loved being together and freely sharing the passion of a new romance.

When the time came to meet her folks, I held my breath.

Her father greeted me at the door, but her mother was hiding in the basement and would not come out as long as I was in the house.

Things went from bad to worse, and the pressure from her family and from friends and old classmates tormented us both. Everybody seemed to know that interracial marriage would hurt our kids and be unfair to them. Dianne and I hung tighter and tighter to each other and finally decided we would marry.

I was then a young student minister at the First Methodist Church in Corvallis, and the folks there were wonderful. The pastor in charge, Ray Balcomb, the minister of music, the District Superintendent and the minister from Dianne's home church all participated in the wedding service. The church's Sanctuary Choir sang a glorious introit and later a festive anthem. The Women's Society for Christian Service (WSCS) provided the food for the reception, and several hundred people joined us in celebrating our vows.

Despite all those preachers, however, nothing could stop Dianne's Uncle Frank from showing up about an hour before the service insisting he be allowed to talk with her. Ray Balcomb cut him off, but Frank would not desist and threatened to disrupt the wedding unless he got to talk with Dianne. Rev. Balcomb convinced him that I was a better target and that he could have ten minutes with me.

Uncle Frank, whom Dianne later said she had no recollection of knowing, ranted at me for every one of those ten minutes. We were condemning our children to a living hell; we were killing Dianne's parents who were broken hearted; we were turning our backs on

friends who really couldn't support interracial marriage; and I was being especially thoughtless and self-
ish not to realize the damage I was doing to Dianne
who would be treated like a whore for marrying a
Negro and would be isolated and subjected to endless
abuse.

As my impatience grew and anger began to flash
its white hot fire in my belly, I found tears rolling from
my eyes. Whenever that happened, I knew I was on the
edge of trying to do my best to kill the culprit causing
the pain. That anger simply could not be subdued by
my commitment to non-violence. I had had enough,
and thankfully, Rev. Balcomb recognized that fact and,
though he was not usually physically demonstrative,
threw his arms around me and invited the dam that
had burst to flow freely into his shoulder.

I cannot remember where Uncle Frank went, but I
knew where I hoped he had landed. Even this intru-
sion could not make our wedding day a disaster.

But a real disaster did strike later when our first
child arrived much earlier than nine months after our
wedding date would have allowed.

I was banned from the pulpit and from participa-
tion in worship services. My role was to meet during
the worship hour with members of the church who
were most upset about the deception regarding our
having had sex before our marriage. I tried to explain
how totally engaged we were with each other and that
the pressures of the interracial debate locked us into

passionate release in each other's arms. I said that we just hoped the pregnancy would last long enough to leave a question mark rather than the exclamation point it did. Most difficult were the questions about "how could you as a minister of the church keep that kind of thing secret?"

This effort at reconciliation was painful beyond description.

I could not undo what I had done, and I knew that the only cure for the deception I had advanced was to be forgiven. No matter how tearful and painfully sincere my request for forgiveness was, it was rejected in visit after visit. There was no forgiveness for a Methodist Minister—especially one who had tricked the church into supporting an interracial marriage conceived in sin. What was the church to do with me?

Methodists do things methodically and by rule, and the "rule book" of the church is in fact called *The Discipline*. So, I endured my purgatory for eight months until June and the Annual Conference arrived. My fate as a Methodist minister hung in the balance. I was in the probationary period Methodists call "on trial" and could have been kicked out of the church. Instead, the ministers, who in my judgment knew how very common my sin was, voted to extend my period of probation for another year. The Bishop would not appoint me and transferred me to the Northern Illinois Conference without consent of the Bishop there, and

Dianne and I left for an inner-city campus ministry in Chicago.

We made our first home on Yale Avenue and later moved to Harvard Avenue in Englewood on Chicago's Southside. Those highbrow street names were indicators of the once glorious suburban character of the now battered inner-city community into which we had moved. St. Barnard's Roman Catholic Church was across the street, and one of the priests there introduced me to the special power Catholics have in Chicago. He took me to the local fire station to play racquetball—a trip you did not enjoy unless your collar was turned backward. Nobody else I came to know even heard of their being racquetball courts in the fire stations in Chicago.

Our apartment building featured a laundry room in the basement, but we would not go there without our dog, Ezekiel—Zeke for short. Zeke loved to chase rats, and he had every opportunity on laundry day. He would catch one and let it go so he could catch it again until the poor thing died of sheer exhaustion or from an unusually rough encounter with one of Zeke's paws. You could almost read the disappointment in Zeke's face when his prey had nothing left and simply laid there. On occasion it was playing possum, and the race around the basement would be on again!

When the minister of Englewood Methodist Church died unexpectedly, I was appointed the interim in addition to my duties at the Campus Christian

Association—an ecumenical student ministry at two commuter schools—Chicago Teachers College (now Chicago State University) and Wilson Junior College (now Kennedy King). We moved into the parsonage on Stewart Avenue next to the church and discovered that the church gym was used by the Englewood Disciples and their street worker, Joe Raymond, for their meetings. I marveled at Joe's fortitude, and only once did I venture out with him to follow up on a cry for help from a gang member whom we later found in an alley dead—with his penis stuck in his mouth. I just could not do that again.

The church gym was still theirs for the using, and Dianne and I came to know a few of the Disciples quite well and did our best to encourage them to find a better life. One night Dianne was late getting home and had taken the CTA train to the Englewood Station. As she departed the station, she noticed someone walking behind her, and she became very nervous and sped along as best she could. Finally making it to the parsonage, she heard a voice behind her say, "Good night, Mrs. Lawrence." It was one of the Disciples who had taken it upon himself to provide her escort service.

Dianne endured Englewood very well indeed. Only once was our home broken into, and only once was one of the kids robbed on his way to the local McDonalds. We walked the neighborhood, shopped and did not think about our safety very much at all.

Not long after the interim appointment to Englewood Church, I was asked to take an interim appointment at Woodlawn Methodist Church—about two miles or so due east. It turned out that my neighbor at the Presbyterian Church there was engaged very deeply with the Blackstone Rangers, the most notorious gang in Chicago at the time and the major rival of the Englewood Disciples. We were frankly somewhat relieved to leave that ministry to the Presbyterians.

Our efforts in Woodlawn were anchored by the strong presence of The Woodlawn Organization (TWO), a Saul Alinsky organization that was in a heated battle with the University of Chicago over their expansion plans. The University seemed oblivious to the needs of their resident neighbors in Woodlawn even though the two neighborhoods were back-to-back and separated only by the famous Midway— home to the 1933 World's Fair and Exposition.

Our family enjoyed the Midway in the winter when the City flooded it for ice skating, and in the spring when its sloping sides provided grassy slides for our kids to roll down onto the flat, park-like promenade.

The Woodlawn Church where I served as interim pastor is gone. Perhaps there was a hint about its future when one Sunday I showed up for worship only to find that someone had taken all the stained glass windows, frames and all.

We later moved on to South Shore where we had our first opportunity to buy a home. This move seemed at the time to be a questionable retreat from our commitment to working in the heart of the City, but I had been "discovered" by Cummins Engine Foundation (CEF) and hired as a Program Officer. We were earning more money than we had ever seen before, and it seemed like a good move because the kids were reaching the age of entry into public school.

Cummins Engine Foundation hired me in 1969 to spend half of my time with four other program officers and the Columbus, Indiana, staff of the Foundation that included Dr. James Joseph and Lt. Gov. Phil Sorensen (Nebraska). We were hired to address the question of why our urban centers were burning following the assassination of Dr. King and direct the foundation's grant budget to help find solutions.

The five program officers wrestled with this very tough assignment until we could agree on a set of proposals we wanted to present to the CEF Board of Trustees chaired by Irwin Miller, Chairman of the Board and Chairman of Cummins Engine Company. Mr. Miller was nominated in the 1960's by *Esquire* magazine as the man most qualified to be President of the United States. He and the other officers of the company were the foundation trustees and engaged us in a very tough debate about how the foundation resources could best be used.

This was only half of the job, and the other half of my time was devoted to continuing to work with Operation Breadbasket and the Englewood Action

Committee in Chicago —volunteer social justice commitments I had made before CEF found me. Cummins saw the importance of its program officers continuing to be engaged as activists and advocates for interracial and economic justice as we wrestled with how to use foundation grant money. They also saw the need to provide each of us with an annual discretionary grant budget of $25,000 that we could use to address small, emergency needs of organizations doing good work in our cities. When CEF made this funding conditional on our moving from our home base to help assure objectivity, each of the black program officers they wanted to hire refused to take the job.

I loved my job. It was the clearly the best job I have ever had, and it continues to be a model of how foundations might structure program officer roles to assure grant making is reality-based. Objectivity isn't all it's cracked up to be, and grant decisions from a safe distance may indeed be safe but also just as likely to be insignificant as vehicles to address the real problem or find the real leadership.

The crisis in our nation's cities was so intense and required so much attention, I did not spend much time at home as I was the first program officer hired and was selected by CEF to coordinate the program in our five cities. My wife, Dianne, bore the weight of rearing the kids and caring for the family's needs. She did a great job, but our relationship was suffering.

A Chicago activist challenged the integrity of the Community Renewal Society's urban-rural exchange program. He had learned that the white participants would not complete the exchange by sending their kids to Chicago although they welcomed black kids from the city to their farms in Wisconsin.

A rift opened between my wife and me, one that would not close. I agreed with the challenge, and my wife did not, and we were never able to settle our differences. I had no idea at the time why this issue was so important to me—nor did my wife. It was the first instance where what mattered to the black community mattered more to me than what mattered to the white community—including my wife.

Only recently have I come to recognize the magnitude of what I was living through as the struggle for integration morphed into the Black Power Movement. The very foundation of my existence was being torn apart. My life had been centered entirely on the "American" part of African-American, and Chicago provided the first immersion for me in a black community—and a black community in chaos. Up to that point in my life I had never had a romantic relationship with a black woman, and I now found myself wrestling with whether I had blocked that possibility out of my life.

One of my colleagues in Woodlawn, Ken Vaughn, was running a program called the School of Human Dignity and enlisted me as a teacher. The basic

message was new to me: Africa is the home of the
human race; African culture was a powerful contrib-
utor to the emergence of civilization; our ancestors
were princes and scholars and architects; our history
has been obliterated and must be recovered. Together
we enlisted members of the community and enrolled
them in class sessions and took this message far and
wide. I was learning about my African ancestors,
and they were amplified by American examples like
DuBois, Woodson, Carver, Booker T. Washington,
Wright, Baldwin and hundreds of others about whom
I had known little or nothing.

Then along came James Forman who challenged
the churches to disperse their wealth among the poor.
Black Methodists for Church Renewal was born. Not
far behind was a drive to increase United Way con-
tributions to black organizations by the development of the National Black United Fund led by my
Los Angeles colleague at Cummins, Walter Bremond.
The Interreligious Foundation for Community
Organization (IFCO) pounded at the National Council
of Churches for a deeper commitment to Africa,
African liberation and the battle against apartheid. In
Chicago, the black police officers organized the first
African-American Patrolmen's League. Even black
foundation officers drew together into the Association
of Black Foundation Executive to explore what special
responsibilities blacks in philanthropy carried.

The last major impact came from a list that was circulated by the Chicago Black Liberation Front on which my name was included as one of the black leaders who should be assassinated because I was married to a white woman.

The world as I knew it was being torn apart, and I was desperate for some stability and reached out to another woman. She was black, and the relationship was intense. Dianne discovered it, and there was no recovery possible.

I was so confused that when at one point Dianne asked me if I ever loved her, I said I didn't know. My hope at that point was that perhaps saying that I never loved her made not loving her now less painful. That was wrong and stupid and cruel although none of those outcomes was intended. I had been head over heels in love with Dianne and joyfully made the trek up the Interstate from Corvallis to Portland to see her as often as I could, and our kids were born in the joy of that love, but my center was lost.

We worked hard to recover our marriage and worked with professionals including clergy, psychiatrists, counselors, and we tried talking with friends— but none could help us repair the damage done by my betrayal. The only hope was forgiveness, and that holy remedy was out of reach.

A MINISTRY OF SOCIAL JUSTICE

I. A MEETIN' WITH THE MAN— MAYOR RICHARD J. DALEY

Mayor Daley, the man widely known as "the Boss," exploded at me. "Nobody comes into this office and demands anything! You weren't elected mayor of this city! Nobody ever elected you to anything." Daley's face reflected his growing anger, and an increasingly deeper red colored his cheeks and nose. Water welled up in his eyes. His hands shook as he launched into a long sermon on the doctrine of citizen subservience to elected officials who represent "all the citizens of Chicago." He did not mention whether they were elected fairly or by a machine that paid its precinct captains with a job and its citizens with a dollar or two for their ballots. My heart sank.

After months of demonstrations and marches in all sorts of weather outside Chicago's City Hall, our Urban Renewal Coalition finally had an appointment in May of 1967 to see Mayor Richard J. Daley.

His mayoral office was huge, and three fully uniformed and armed Chicago policemen guarded the reception area. One of the officers had escorted us into a conference room and announced that the mayor would join us shortly. Daley himself strode in just moments later and without preamble asked, "What can I do for you?"

Everything went along fine at first. Coalition members discussed the composition of their community council, and then one of the members of the delegation "demanded" that the mayor consider the names the delegation had brought. That's when Daley exploded.

When the mayor paused to gasp for air, I tried my best to be a peacemaker and hurriedly interjected, "Mr. Mayor, I am sure my friend did not mean to say that he could demand you do anything. His words simply show how strongly he feels about the people who decide what happens in his neighborhood."

Daley turned abruptly, pointed his finger at me and bellowed, "And is this the kind of leadership you listen to? Is this the kind of person you want on your community conservation council? Because this man doesn't know anything about urban renewal. This is a man who would force his way into City Council and disrupt the meetings of our Aldermen. You want me to appoint men like that to run urban renewal?"

The delegation shot back a few weak "yesses" to the mayor's questions, and as they recovered from the shock and tension, joined with increasingly forceful voices in a mixed chorus of "yes, yes we do, yes we do!"

"Well then, tell me, what do you know about urban renewal, Reverend?"

The last word was cold as a curse. My anger, though slow to boil, was starting to bubble up. I shot back, "I know that in Englewood on the Southside where I live, you're tearing down 826 units of good housing to make parking lots for your friends at Chicago City Bank and their business buddies. Parking lots to 'insulate' white shoppers from the black residents who live in our community. Parking lots for businesses and nothing for the people."

The mayor laughed derisively. "You see. He doesn't know what he's talking about. He doesn't know how much housing we've built in Englewood. Just ask him. Just ask him. How many housing units have we built in Englewood, Reverend?"

"None in the Central Englewood Project Area." My answer was blurred after the "none" as the mayor once again filled the room with his scornful laughter. "He doesn't know what he's talking about. I told you he doesn't know what he's talking about. We've built over 200 new homes in Englewood..."

"Two hundred built doesn't make up for 826 torn down." This time I interrupted him. "And I'm talking about Central Englewood around Sears and Chicago City Bank. And in that project area there were NO HOMES BUILT—just parking lots. Is that your idea of urban renewal, mister mayor? A housing program with no housing? A 'renewal' program that destroys good housing?" Nothing could stop either one of us, and the shouting became increasingly louder. "You can't make me do anything," the mayor screamed pointing at me again, "and if this is your idea of leadership…"

"Mr. Mayor. Mr. Mayor, please. My leadership is not the issue. This delegation has a list of names and would like to address the qualities and qualifications these people have to offer."

But the mayor would not hear it. "You don't know what you're talking about, Reverend. You don't know anything about urban renewal, and you have misled these people. You say we haven't built any homes in Englewood, and you're a liar."

I was stunned. Even my clerical collar failed to connect with Daley's Roman Catholic tradition and his reputed respect for the clergy. My stomach churned, and my whole body shook in frustration. I knew tears of anger were welling in my eyes as I fought for self-control. Words echoed in my head, but they seemed inadequate.

My inability to respond was finally relieved when one of the men in the group took leadership into his own hands and began to speak about the names on our list. When he was finished and started to walk forward to hand the list to the mayor, the burly police officer abruptly stopped him and insisted he take the list for the mayor.

Our appointment was over. The mayor turned without looking back at us and walked through the door into his inner office. If he looked at our list, it apparently was only to make sure the crumpled ball made it into his wastebasket. He did not appoint a single person we had suggested.

It is amazing that a man who ignored the pleas of the public could ever be elected, but Richard J. Daley had not been elected mayor of Chicago on his personality or his temperament. He was elected because he was a master of machine politics. When we could no longer stand the injustices created by the Daley machine, we joined a lawsuit brought by the Independent Voters of Illinois. It charged that it was illegal to force city workers to do political work, make financial contributions and tie their employment to meeting quotas needed to win political campaigns.

To our great surprise, we won!

It is true that my face-to-face peacemaking attempt did not win us true urban renewal during Richard Daley's lifetime. Our nonviolent victory took another form. Perseverance and patience working within the system put a limp in the haughty stride of the Daley machine, a limp that would eventually cripple its ability to keep up with the changing times. Sixteen years later in 1983, after Richard J. Daley had died in office, Harold Washington, the first independent, African-American mayor in the history of the City of Chicago, galloped to victory.

I wonder if the new life, hope, opportunities and jobs created by the election of Harold Washington for thousands of residents who had been "outsiders" in Daley's Chicago, created a little jealousy in Mayor Richard J. Daley. Chicagoans celebrated their victory in electing "Harold, Harold, Harold!" with genuine joy. They gave Mayor Washington an enthusiastic and affectionate endorsement which Daley's machine had never produced for "the Boss." Mayor Washington received a special gift that the people withheld from Mayor Daley, because that gift is reserved for winners and losers who are loved, not feared.

SOCIAL JUSTICE MINISTRY II: DR. MARTIN LUTHER KING, JR. COMES TO THE SOUTHSIDE

> *I've been in many demonstrations all across the*
> *   South,*
> *but I can say that I have never seen, even in*
> *   Mississippi and Alabama,*
> *mobs as hostile and as hate-filled as I've seen in*
> *   Chicago.*

> Dr. Martin Luther King, Jr.,
> Chicago, 1966

We tried everything to stop the urban renewal project at 63rd and Halsted in Englewood on Chicago's
Southside.

It was hard to believe that a project that proposed to
tear down housing of which eighty percent was standard—NOT sub-standard—NOT blighted. The main
idea was to provide space for a perimeter of parking
lots for the businesses in what had suddenly become
a black community. Chicago's segregated neighborhoods changed fast once the move from white to black
was initiated—and especially so if there was block
busting going on by greedy real estate salespeople
who fed the fears of white homeowners about the im-
minent decline of property values when blacks moved
into their neighborhood. Realtors then made a "last
chance" offer to the frightened homeowners and sold
it to hungry black buyers at exorbitant prices. If the
panic wasn't sufficient, agents would buy a home and
arrange for a black family to move onto the block on
the border between the black and white neighborhoods. Whites fled taking what little they could get.

White flight made the business owners at 63rd
and Halsted very nervous. White shoppers were
afraid of coming back to shop in their old neighborhood, so the local business leaders put together their
very own Englewood Planning Association and a
phony neighborhood group called the Englewood
Community Organization (ECO) to support a

massive urban renewal project. ECO was headed by a black minister who would not hear our pleas to oppose the business interests' plan to displace black families who had only recently bought into their homes—and then only on land contract as regular bank mortgages were not available to blacks.

We tried to take over the ECO at their annual meeting, but they outsmarted us with a parliamentary move that made two-thirds of the community members who had joined ineligible to vote.

So, we organized the Englewood Action Committee as an opposing voice for the community. One of our member organizations, the Green Street Association, wanted to sue the City, so we helped raise money to launch their lawsuit. It went all the way to the U.S. Supreme Court[1] only to have the Court rule against the local homeowners.

Since the previous summer had produced so much violence and tension over the open housing marches led by Dr. King, we decided to organize a caravan for the black homeowners to look for new homes in the white areas of SW Chicago. We really did not dare go back to Gage Park where the violence had been fiercest, so we designated a community called Beverly Hills. Again we were outdone. Chicago police were

---

[1] Green Street Association, et al. v. Richard J. Daley, 250 F. Supp. 139 (N.D. Ill. 1966).

everywhere, and no one was on the streets, so the day went by without an ugly confrontation of any kind. It did not make the major media news outlets and only attracted coverage by the Chicago Defender, the black newspaper.

Christmas was approaching, and we decided to organize a boycott of the businesses at 63 and Halsted. We had supported Operation Breadbasket in pickets of grocery stores that resulted in negotiating of covenants that captured a wide range of jobs and business for blacks, Latinos and women.

The Action Committee met every week on Sunday after church to finalize plans for the Christmas Boycott and decided we would blow up black helium balloons with a big red STOP sign printed on them and a leaflet that read: "Santa Says Do Not Shop at 63rd and Halsted this Christmas." The flyer told the story of the urban renewal project and the loss of homes by the black families who made up the Green Street Association. We had black Santas and pickets—many in rented Santa Claus suits—on all four blocks of the major intersection every day for two long weeks, but the shoppers took our balloons and went on into the Sears and the other stores to buy their Christmas gifts. The cold weather took its toll, and our numbers dwindled.

Our meetings were usually high-spirited, but all of us were tired, discouraged and depressed. Since I was the chairman, I tried to help the group with one suggestion after another of possible actions to increase our effectiveness. One of our members, a young college student active with the Student CORE (Congress on Racial Equality) chapter at Chicago Teachers College, interrupted and made comments that were consistently negative and very difficult to take. Finally I asked him if he had a suggestion, and he answered, "Yeah, I've got a suggestion. I move that you resign so someone who knows the black community can run things. You are ignorant and a pale excuse for a black leader."

My reserve was gone, and I dashed across the circle of chairs and swung a violent left hook at him that ripped the sleeve out of my Sunday suit at the armpit. He stepped inside its arc, and I grabbed him by the neck trying to choke the life out of him. He had hit two soft spots: I am an extremely light-complexioned African-American and being called "ignorant" was an insult more painful for me than any other for some reason.

The Rev. John Porter, a Methodist preacher committed to engaging his congregation with issues of social justice and whose church served as the Southside home for Chicago's Southern Christian Leadership Conference (SCLC), jumped between us shouting, "Brother Lawrence. Brother Lawrence. Please. Please", while he pulled my fingers away from the young agitator's throat.

My eyes were flowing with tears of anger that served to inspire my accuser to laugh at me. I continued to struggle to get at him, but several other committee members were now pulling us apart.

When we reconvened I offered to resign, but the group would not hear of it, and the excitement had sparked a new surge of energy. Someone suggested we organize the churches that had accounts in the bank at 63rd and Halsted to march from Rev. Porter's church and make a mass withdrawal. There was even a burst of humor as someone else suggested that the total withdrawal would surely break the bank. The bank president, Norbert Engels, was the chief advocate of the urban renewal plan and served as chair of the city-wide Urban Renewal Conservation Committee.

We were excited and energized and went to work calling preachers and lined up about two dozen for the big day. Our final meeting on the day of the march was interrupted by an announcement by Rev. Porter. "Dr. King is coming!" Dr. King was living on the Westside, and we did not get to see much of him.

The words were as cheerful as the news that Santa Claus was on the roof. Folks buzzed and chatted and smiled as we informally talked over the final arrangements for the demonstration. We had followed the discipline of the movement and met with Mr. Engels and asked him to support our demand that the urban renewal plan be scrapped.

We also noticed that his bank reflected the racial realities in Chicago—a reality that had moved Dr. King to make Chicago his home base to fight segregated housing. Nearly all the bank customers were African-American, while nearly all its employees were whites. An integrated financial institution was as rare in Chicago as was an integrated neighborhood. Chicago deserved its ranking as one of the most segregated cities in the nation because of a clear line between the black and white communities—a dangerous line for either group to cross.

White fear of shopping in the black neighborhood around the bank caused the business owners to panic. Since they could not move their businesses, the owners, including Sears-Roebuck, decided to take the property of black homeowners, tear it down and create a "safety perimeter" of parking lots hoping it would assure white shoppers it was safe to come back to the old neighborhood. To make matters worse, these white business owners used urban renewal and taxpayers' money to insulate themselves from a community of black residents they did not trust and whose business they did not solicit.

Our boycott of the businesses there and their leader, Norbert Engels, the bank president, a very well connected Texan, and a friend and political ally of both President Lyndon B. Johnson and Chicago Mayor Richard J. Daley, had little impact.

Now we had the news that Dr. King was coming to join us in our demonstration, and as chairperson of the Englewood Action Committee and one of the boycott organizers, I couldn't be happier. We all wanted to work directly with the great civil rights leaders for a very long time after the long summer of open housing marches.

Finally, Dr. King and his assistants made their way into the church basement, and after shaking hands all around, Dr. King turned to me and said, "All right now, Reverend Lawrence, what's the plan for the day?"

I was caught a little off guard and stumbled and mumbled as I tried to collect my thoughts. I had just assumed Dr. King would take over the leadership of this demonstration by some magical power. Rather than accept the omnipotence with which we had endowed him, he reminded me and the clergy from the community gathered "to do justice" that we were the real leaders and the real heroes. "You have been fighting this battle for a long time, and I am more than ready and willing to follow your leadership," he said. "Tell me what you want me to do."

I told him we had worn ourselves out picketing in the cold of winter, and we were tired of being ignored. I did not exaggerate when I added that his presence that day was a blessing beyond measure. We wanted to find a way to get the bank president's attention, and I thought the best way to do it was to march in our clerical robes from the very church where we were meeting and withdraw our church accounts.

I also explained that the Reverend John Porter had opened the doors of his sanctuary to serve as the foundation for the fight for freedom on the Southside of Chicago. He had led our boycott in a bright red Santa Claus outfit on many days that winter and handed out hundreds of black balloons and leaflets. I thanked Reverend Porter, who stood and acknowledged the applause and shouts with a smile before retreating from the group.

I continued to speak: "We are trying to stop this urban renewal project which is tearing down good housing which blacks have to buy on land contract because banks will not make mortgage loans to us. They are replacing that housing with parking lots for their businesses. Yes! I said parking lots," I shouted, and the congregation of clergy moaned and muttered, "Oh Lord. Oh Lord."

Rev. Porter quietly stepped back into the room. He had put on his Santa suit and walked forward to give Dr. King a black balloon and a leaflet with the facts about the 63rd and Halsted Urban Renewal Project. Dr. King smiled and accepted the tokens.

But the unity in the room was about to dissipate. Rev. Stroy Freeman, who was the pastor of one of the larger churches on the Southside, rose from the back to say he could not support a protest march to the bank in which the clergy wore their clerical robes.

I wondered if the magic of Dr. King's presence could have evaporated so quickly. The answer was immediate and obvious. A number of clergy joined in a spontaneous and heated debate. Dr. King was silent, although I thought I saw a look of impatience from one of his lieutenants, the Reverend Bernard Lee.

But it was James Orange, a field worker for the Southern Christian Leadership Conference (SCLC)— the religious, organizational and political entity behind Dr. King—who broke through the chaos. "I have been stoned and spit upon here in Chicago, and the car I was riding in with Rev. Lawrence to join our march in Gage Park was nearly turned over on last Tuesday and was later set on fire," James said. "In Gage Park they don't care if you're a preacher or a pimp or the President of SCLC. We need to stand tall as a people who are hated in this city for no reason other than the color of our skin. But more than that, we need our preachers to stand tall for justice." James bowed his head and paused, "As long as we are willing to stand tall, who cares what we're wearing?" Only then did I recognize that James Orange was dressed in the bib-style overalls of the plantation farmhand.

Dr. King followed with another, even more troubling question for the group. "What should we expect today as we go out to this bank? Are the police planning to stop us and arrest us on the way, or will they arrest us as we line up in the bank to withdraw our money? Will we face those White Power counter-demonstrators we have come to know so well in Gage Park?"

A somber silence filled the room. We had not anticipated everything that might happen, especially the possible threats the forces of reaction would present. And it was true: we might be stepping out into an unknown filled with unexpected and ugly goblins.

"We have nothing to fear," Dr. King reassured us. "It's just that wherever I go in Chicago, I find myself facing crowds more hostile than those I've encountered anywhere else in the nation. And we need to be ready." He reminded us about the principles of non-violent action and asked Rev. James Bevel to rehearse with us the disciplines required. Then he set out the challenge: "We need to try to talk with this bank president and give him one more chance to respond to our demands to do justice and respect our community. And if he does not listen, then we must proceed to take our money away from him."

A long silence followed, a testimony to the impact that Dr. King as our teacher and leader had upon us. There were soft murmurs of "Amen" and "Thank you, Lord." "I want to remind you of a story from the New Testament, the one in which Peter asks Jesus: 'Lord, do I really have to forgive those who do me wrong seven times?'" Dr. King's message built gradually on this theme, and as it grew in magnitude and volume, the preachers responded with urgings to "Tell it, Martin. Preach, Brother Martin." More voices called in a rising chorus of "Amen" and "Yes, Lord." Dr. King abandoned his carefully articulated and measured academic tones and cried out with rhythmic, poetic pleadings, as his audience worked with him to deliver and affirm the word.

Even I, a black man refined in the white culture of the United Methodist tradition, rocked in my seat and offered my own subdued affirmations with "Yes-s-s-s. Yes-s-s-s-s, Yes-s-s-s-s."

Smiles of joy and victory danced on the faces of everyone present as we rose into the ranks of God's mighty army of righteous warriors. We knew we were going to overcome some day. Even if we lost this battle, we would sit together at the feet of the Almighty and share in the blessing of having suffered and died trying to do the right thing. Nothing could stop us now.

We could not go much higher. We had reached a pinnacle and were ready to march forward, when suddenly Dr. King dropped his head. He offered no words at all for several moments, and the shouting and joy quietly left the room. A profound sense of anticipation told us something great was about to happen.

Dr. King spoke quietly, "I tell you, my brothers, that we must not indulge in hatred, but we must learn to forgive those who have done harm to us. Not seven times, but seventy times seven." "Our march today is not a march on Chicago City Bank," he continued. "It is a march for truth and justice, a march for jobs and respect. We do not march on the bank president, Mr. Engels. We march on all those evil impulses for greed which have captured him and so many like him and turned them into scavengers who feed upon the weak in our society and use federal programs like Urban Renewal for purposes for which they were never designed."

"And when we march today, we must march together proudly as children of God, hating no one, cursing no one, condemning no one. Let us march together, brethren, and let us not get weary. For the day is coming when we shall all see a great Light and bask in the warmth of the glory of the Son of God who will wrap his loving arms around us and give us that home we have fought for and failed to find here on the Southside of Chicago. And it shall be a home where there is no mortgage, for our debts have all been paid. And now, let us all say 'Amen.'"

Dr. King turned to me. "Reverend Lawrence, are you ready?"

My reply was louder and bolder than I had any right to expect, "Dr. King, we are ready."

"Then lead on, Brother Lawrence."

Immediately after agreeing to the challenge from Dr. King, a procession of pastors led by Dr. King and I strode peacefully toward Chicago City Bank and Trust. Clergy and their followers all approached the tellers and withdrew whatever amount of money they had in the bank.

Someone joked, "We'd better call Brinks to protect us with all this money!"

While waiting on the sidewalk for everyone to finish the transactions, James Orange, SCLC staffer and friend, suggested we burn my bankbook as a symbolic end to the demonstration. Dr. King agreed, and the photographer from the *Daily Defender,* John Gunn, snapped this picture.

If you look closely under the street sign, you just might be able to find the flicker of a flame that marked the making of an historic day for Dr. King and me and the other Englewood Action Committee's fighters for justice.

III. REV. JESSE JACKSON TEACHES US PREACHERS ABOUT ECONOMIC JUSTICE

I walked out of the special meeting of the Ministers of Operation Breadbasket hurt, angry and no longer able to hold back the flood of tears of disappointment and pain. The ministers of Operation Breadbasket loved the Rev. Jesse Jackson, and so did I. I worked tirelessly to support Jesse's leadership of Breadbasket, a program of the Southern Christian Leadership Conference. Dr. King had installed Jesse in Chicago as the Breadbasket leader. Rev. Jackson was young in comparison to many of the local clergy who supported him, but he found ways to teach and work among us in powerful ways that moved preachers out of their pulpits and into the streets—not a common sight. He rewarded us with his personal blessings and public acknowledgment in the massive Saturday morning Breadbasket meetings. He hailed our role as the chief agents responsible for the detailed research needed to successfully negotiate covenants to increase minority employment with major employers in Chicago.

I became Chair of the Ministers Negotiating Committee, and we did the research that identified the worst offenders among the grocery stores that filled the "breadbaskets" in our community. We mobilized the picket lines that were the key to our strategy of economic justice by withholding our dollars from our neighborhood villains. We were not at all certain that we could say "boycott" without being charged with illegally interfering with the freedom to do business, but boycott is surely what we organized, and they were effective.

Rev. Jackson had helped us put content into our general concerns about justice. He contended that ministers could and should lead the boycott because ministers in the community were those whose motives could not be challenged in confronting the retail giants to win jobs. We would gain nothing personally from the commitments we struck. In fact, our promissory note was called a "covenant," a biblical reference to sacred promises between the employer and the community.

Our discipline required that we first educate ourselves about the company we were trying to confront, and several of us spent hours with staff assistance researching the company's strengths, weaknesses, and numbers of stores in the black community compared to their total operations. We learned about the profit margins in the grocery business which helped to inform us about how tough the struggle would be.

We then informed the company of what we had found and asked for a meeting to discuss resolution of what we saw as an obvious injustice. It was clear that the black community did not have proportionate representation among the employees the company had hired nor did black-owned businesses represent a reasonable share of the company's suppliers.

If the company agreed to reform its operations to address the injustice we had uncovered, or if they supplied additional information and remained in good faith negotiations with the Negotiating Committee, the talks continued. If the company ignored our request, we would send a certified letter indicating that failure to discuss and address the issues we had identified was cause for us to determine whether we should encourage members of the black community and others who supported our goals for proportionate hiring, which we called distributive justice, to shop at other grocery stores. We would put together a flyer with a summary of the facts and organize an informational picket line and encourage blacks to withdraw their business until a covenant had been reached and a return to the targeted grocery was justified.

Getting a covenant with National Foods was a major battle for us. They failed to answer our most recent letter demanding additional information on the hiring of blacks and their use of minority-owned businesses. So, a small delegation of the members of the Breadbasket Negotiating Committee was seated in the corporate offices demanding a meeting with the president. Our visits and visual counts of the employees in National's stores in the black community showed that only five to six percent of the employees were black—even though the stores were located in neighborhoods where they were surrounded by blacks and were supported by shoppers who were nearly all black.

We found that in the district and corporate offices like the one we were in, the numbers were even worse. We had asked National to work with us to recognize this disparity and to identify and commit to change what they were doing and create a plan to address the inequity. The "covenant"—a signed promissory document signed at a Saturday morning Breadbasket meeting—was required to detail the number of intended new black employees. It would also show how and when blacks would be hired in what numbers at all levels in the company. The Ministers of Operation Breadbasket expected National Foods would agree that, as a corporate citizen, it needed a plan to deal with our concern. There simply was not a sufficient number of black employees present in the workforce in their stores relative to the numbers of blacks in the population who shopped there.

National Foods did not believe we were serious about negotiating our differences, so the company chose to ignore our request for a meeting. We had come to their offices anyway believing that there was nothing more important to a responsible corporate citizen than an issue of justice and that the company officers would make time for an appointment with us. We were prepared to stay as long as necessary. Some might call it a sit-in.

Our negotiating team felt a strength we had never experienced before or since—a strength that rested in the fact that we had power. We were really negotiating, because we had proven that we could organize an informational picket line that would effectively turn away ninety to ninety-five percent of the customers at any store where we were present. We knew National Foods and other grocery chains' margins could not tolerate that loss of business.

Our Ministers Negotiating Committee had written and informed National Foods that we planned to come to their offices if they did not respond, and they were ready—not for a meeting, but for a confrontation. That was easily recognized when we were approached by a person in a uniform—the chief security officer for the company—who announced that we were on private property and that we were trespassing and must leave in five minutes or the Chicago police would be called and we would be arrested.

Rev. Jackson did all the talking. He reiterated our desire for a meeting with the president of National Foods and reaffirmed our intention to stay right where we were until we got one. When he was finished, he turned to our delegation and asked, "Rev. Lawrence, Brother Forshey, are you ready to go to jail for Breadbasket to advance the cause of economic justice?"

It was time to stand up and be counted. What could I say? I had been arrested before. The first time was a sit-in in the middle of State and Jackson Streets in the Loop in downtown Chicago. Dick Gregory was leading a protest of the racist practices of Superintendent of Chicago public schools, Benjamin Willis, who erected portable classrooms (we called them "Willis wagons") in the playgrounds around black schools to keep black children segregated, even after we had proven to the court that empty classrooms were available in nearby white schools.

On one other occasion, I had led a protest against a Chicago police officer named Burleigh Ginkle who had stopped a vehicle on a traffic offense and ended up shooting and killing the driver, Richard Franklin Hagan, a black father and former sparring partner of Joe Louis. Hagan had his child with him in the car, and the officer supposedly saw Hagan reaching for a weapon, fired his own gun and killed him.

When no disciplinary action was scheduled by the Chicago Police Department, we decided to organize a protest at the officer's home in Gage Park, a section of Chicago where fiery demonstrations had flared all summer.

Our plan was to kneel on the sidewalk in a prayer vigil after knocking on the officer's door and inviting him to join us in prayer. Once the doorbell rang, police officers descended from everywhere. James Orange of SCLC and I were arrested for disorderly conduct and interfering with a police officer. I was so angry about the injustice of my arrest and conviction that I spent 20 days in jail in Chicago rather than pay the $100 fine.

We fought this case and went all the way to the U. S. Supreme Court and petitioned Justice Thurgood Marshall on a writ of habeas corpus to set me free. The law under which I had been arrested was struck down after my arrest by a Federal Court, but somehow that didn't matter to the Supreme Court in Illinois. Despite my attorney's assurances that the request for a writ would result in my release in "a day or two at most", I found myself in jail.

I am never ready to go to jail. I am afraid of what goes on in there, but I assumed Rev. Jackson would be going with us, so I boldly announced that I was ready. I think the other minister, Rev. Gerald Forshey, a fellow Methodist, thought the same thing. Jesse told us that he could not be arrested that day because he needed "to take the message of what went on here today to the flock," so we had prayer, and the Chicago police arrived and asked the delegation to leave or face arrest. Only the two of us designated for jail stayed, and we were arrested.

As the hours crept along and no one appeared with bond money, we were transferred from the district police station to central lockup downtown, booked and arraigned before a judge. I finally got a chance to use my free call and contacted my wife who eventually raised the $200 bail needed to set us both free.

The following Saturday we were treated like heroes at the Operation Breadbasket meeting, a meeting that feels like church but is like none other. It is the typical black church in one way—loud and moving music by the youth choir and the breadbasket choir, great preaching with shouts and whooping and lots of prayer. But Breadbasket had what no other church offered—a major dose of social action tied to its regular celebrations. It was not unusual at all for us to leave the Saturday morning Breadbasket meeting and march to the local store where picket lines were established to support our demands for jobs and justice.

I expected that on this particular Saturday after our arrest, National Foods Company would feel the full wrath of the Ministers of Breadbasket, but I was surprised to learn that Rev. Jackson would not join us on the picket line because he had received word of a major crisis. He and Dr. Robert Thomas, chair of the medical division of Operation Breadbasket who was also Jesse's personal physician, would lead a march on Englewood Hospital.

I was shocked and disappointed.

Rev. Jackson asked for folks to stay and follow my directions to the National food stores targeted for today's picketing. I knew better, and there was a hollow ring to the announcement. I could not avoid the feeling in my stomach that I had been betrayed—or at least abandoned.

Very few folks went anywhere other than where Jesse went. He was the leader. Everyone loved him and wanted to be near him and watch him perform the magic of his personal power on the enemy of the day. He was electric, and I cannot recall one single occasion when Jesse came away from a confrontation of this sort that he did not come away a winner. So, who is going to stay and picket with me?

Surprisingly, a small contingent did stay and met me in the foyer of the Breadbasket meeting hall. I distributed the picket signs I had made after being released from jail, and we went over information on the leaflet we were distributing that day, rehearsed the discipline required on the picket line, answered any questions, identified the picket captains and gave out the assignment sheets.

We had enough people to picket effectively at two stores, but I had prepared material for every one of

National stores in our community and was certain that massive picket lines would send a clear message of how powerful and determined Breadbasket was about earning respect for the demands of its Ministers Negotiations Committee.

When I got home I wrote a letter to Rev. Jackson and the Ministers of Operation Breadbasket expressing my feelings of disappointment about a lack of organizational focus and discipline. I argued that we could not win these battles if we were going to take on every crisis that emerged in the community, and that we had to get Rev. Jackson's commitment to negotiations and the follow-up required as a first priority.

In addition, I complained that we had simply not done a good job of follow-up on the agreements which we called covenants, and everyone on Breadbasket's Steering Committee knew we needed a team to track how well the companies were doing at meeting the hiring goals and other targets contained in those covenants. If the companies were not doing well, that team should recommend further picketing and the resumption of the boycott of that company to remind them that we were serious and retained our power. This was not a charade. This was a step on the road toward distributive justice, the beginning of the march for economic justice. The cause was just and right, and timing was everything. The time for measured progress in this arena was long overdue, and Breadbasket had an ability and power few organizations had ever displayed.

No one would have said a thing to me or done anything if I had stopped there, but instead of leaving it as a sermon to the organization, I added a single line which was prompted by my fascination with the true impact of power. I added: "Failure to shape the organization along the lines I have described will result in my going to the media and detailing the covenants we had made and the failings of the companies to meet those commitments and our failure to have done anything about those broken agreements."

It worked.

Rev. Jackson had never called me personally for anything, and although I often got calls from his office about meetings, I was shocked and surprised to hear his voice on the other end of the phone asking me to attend a special Ministers Steering Committee meeting the next day. I readily agreed and felt vindicated, powerful and hopeful that the organization was ready to change.

My arrival at the Steering Committee quickly erased all hope. The ministers of Operation Breadbasket were already assembled, had an agenda of other business which they interrupted upon my arrival and directed me to an empty chair inside the circle their chairs created. There was no sign of Rev. Jackson, but the Rev. Clay Evans, Chair of the Steering Committee, opened the issue for discussion by reading my letter. When he was done he looked at me and said words to the effect, "Rev. Lawrence, this is a wonderful letter, and we all know how hard you've worked for Operation Breadbasket." There was a long pause before he continued. "But we cannot tolerate a traitor to the cause of freedom. And God knows there is a special and eternal place in hell for those who attack our leaders. Rev. Jackson is the leader of Operation Breadbasket—not you. Neither you nor I can tell him what to do. I would not think of trying to tell him what to do. He marches to orders from the Almighty, and it is our job to follow his leadership. I must know whether you will pledge full faith and service to the cause of freedom, and I must know whether you will remove your ugly threat to take our business to the press."

One after the other the members of the Steering Committee commented in a similar vein, and while my fury grew, so did my resolve. I would have nothing more to do with this organization. I would not be abused and insulted and disrespected. I had no personal agenda and was interested only in making Breadbasket more effective. And I knew that nothing would be done and nothing would change if Rev. Jackson was not present. So, I withheld any response of any kind. I also held back the tears which welled up in my eyes, and I listened and wept silently, secretly grieving over the loss of the truest opportunity I had ever participated in to make up for a significant part of the unfair employment practices of the past.

I left the meeting without saying a word.

I could not keep my resolve to stay away, however, because there simply was nothing better going on in the community at the time. Even though I thought the transformation of Breadbasket into Operation PUSH, (People United to Save Humanity) by Rev. Jackson on Christmas Eve was a subtle allusion to his special place in God's eyes, I was drawn back into the organization anyway. However, I could not deliver the resolve, the commitment or the intensity of effort I once mustered so easily. I had been badly hurt by the Ministers Steering Committee's "circle of justice" and was clearly still suspect.

When I decided to run for a vacant seat on the City Council in Chicago, Operation Breadbasket failed to endorse my candidacy in the special election in the summer of 1972. Yet, when Jesse ran for president in 1984, I felt a special pride in working in Portsmouth, New Hampshire distributing literature and helping the Massachusetts Jackson for President Campaign Coordinator with fundraising. There was a special charge to my voting in that presidential primary and having the chance to support a black candidate I knew and a candidate I had worked with and loved.

The next time I saw Rev. Jackson, he was in Seattle on a speaking engagement trying to energize the Washington State Rainbow Coalition. I tried to get his office to schedule some time somewhere so I could invite my son, Benjamin, to meet him. That failed to materialize, so we decided to crash the Rainbow meeting at Mount Zion Baptist Church. When Rev. Jackson saw me there, he grabbed me in a fond embrace and reminded me of how long we had worked together. He then delivered a speech that was vintage Jesse Jackson, and I rocked and remembered how eloquently and creatively passionate he could be and how powerful and incisive his one-liners could be, such as, "We only need one Republican party in this country no matter what Bill Clinton may think." I was proud of him and was reminded again of just how gigantic a man he really is. He has given much to become the first serious African-American candidate for President of the United States in the history of this country.

Right on, Jesse!

LIGHT, BRIGHT, DAMN NEAR WHITE

During my days at Albion College, I spent the 1956 Thanksgiving holiday break with my college roommate in the suburb of Royal Oak, Michigan. When we arrived at his home, his father came hurriedly down the stairs to greet us with the news that he was late because "he just had to finish a great book which proved beyond a shadow of a doubt that gorillas are superior to Negroes."

I stood dumbfounded and silent, and so did my roommate, who then proceeded to introduce me to his dad whose hand I shook without saying a word, because in those days I did not do anything to disturb a white person in hopes that my tolerance would help to bridge the gap between the races.

The pain of that encounter has been multiplied many times over in my life and magnified when other blacks are certain that I am not an African-American. I had heard and truly hoped that blacks did recognize other blacks no matter how light we might be.

Another myth just crashed, and I lived within no "natural" tribe and suffered the indignities blacks and whites liberally cast upon each other.

Naturally, I tried to date, but despite the lightness of my complexion, when relationships with girls moved toward a level of seriousness, the girls somehow knew there was danger on the horizon and sounded an alarm.

So, when I fell in love with a white grad student during my days at the University of Chicago and asked her to marry me, I learned how far these warning signals traveled. After she accepted and told her parents, they first tried to deflect her affection with the offer of a long trip to Europe—all expenses paid if she would stop seeing me. Debbie was an Art History major and had longed to see the art museums in Europe, but what had once been a promise upon graduation, now became a bribe. Then, the parents insisted that we see a marriage counselor of their choosing, who in her "professional opinion" concluded we were crazy to continue to think we could be happy in an interracial marriage. Finally, Debbie's parents threatened to commit her to a mental institution if she did not end the relationship, and she eventually caved in.

As a younger man, to help make myself acceptable to whites, I had no reservations about trying to cover any remaining "blemishes" of being black that had somehow survived the battle of the genes. I grew up in all-white Ballardvale, MA—part of the fairly well-known Town of Andover. I did everything I could to avoid being black: I straightened my hair for church and other special occasions; was careful not to be loud; I had no love for a Cadillac; I used lots of deodorant and I did not dance—although one of the stereotypes about being black I could not give up: I loved music and sang a lot. My unquestioned commitment to doing whatever was required to make myself acceptable to whites had nearly no limit in those early days of my life.

My efforts set off subtle rumblings of resentment from some darker-complexioned blacks I met at Third Baptist Church in Lawrence, MA (I've never found the First and Second Baptist Churches) where members of our family would worship on occasion. I later learned that those blacks felt I displayed a cold superiority in my "proper" demeanor.

I thought their coldness was really jealousy. I believed deeply that all of us who were black hungered to be accepted by whites, and there was no doubt in those days that the lighter you were, the better your chances of winning acceptance.

I began to look around to test an assertion I'd heard that black men dated and married only black women who were lighter-complexioned than they. My observations proved the assertion to be accurate, and exceptions to the rule were rare.

It was a long time before I learned how completely the terror that is racism had impacted me and other blacks in America. Not only had the brutality of slavery, lynching, and segregation supported by law and law enforcers robbed us of our freedom and self-esteem, those devils had stolen our humanity. The viciousness of the enforcement of racism taught blacks that we will dance when we're told to do so even when there is no music, that we will smile when there is nothing funny and that we will treat our superiors with respect even when nothing about them deserves respect. Those commandments buried themselves deep into each of us, so we never learned to be free to be ourselves—only to be what was demanded of us. We were taught to fear what the repercussions of disobedience would be and hated ourselves because we did not dare to hate our oppressor.

I thought the only choice I had was to be everything the white man expected of me, and that my success would be reflected by my being able to date and marry a white woman—which I did.

My marriage and my commitment to integration were rocked by a growing rage and a sense of black consciousness that blossomed following the assassination of Dr. King. I found myself mesmerized in the Temple of Islam in Chicago listening to the rhetoric of Black Muslim preachers. I was totally perplexed by the good feelings and the curiously powerful pull of the call to "truth, justice and freedom" under the crescent of Islam pictured in a huge mural hung behind the podium. Christianity was represented in that mural as a stark black tree with large limbs from one of which a black person was hanging lynched. The confusion generated by the call to be "free, black and proud" caused my marriage to spiral out of control and end in a devastating divorce. I did not know how to love myself and love a white woman too, and I gave up trying to hold together a family I loved deeply. I caused my kids and my wife to get on without me because the load I carried was impossible to bear and nearly dropped me to my knees.

My light complexion and my experiences growing up in the white community of Andover meant I lived on the boundary between the cultures and the colors that dominate the American landscape. For it was the school department in Andover that was responsible for my education--that same school department later rejected my sister Cynthia's application for a teaching position upon her graduation from Boston State Teachers College in 1960 because, "Andover was not ready for a black teacher." I can only speculate about what damage an education in the Andover schools had done to me and the other black family in town.

I know that Andover enabled me to be at ease in the white community, but never really able to be at home there—or anywhere.

Some whites, without having been asked, try to comfort me with "but you're not really black." It is as if they are doing me a favor with their personal emancipation proclamations. They are not aware that I hunger to be black and to discover where my ancestral connections are and to be able to go home and learn about ancestors with whom I cannot connect now other than knowing they were slaves from some country likely on the western coast of Africa. How my father got to Nova Scotia is a great mystery, and while other blacks can travel to the South and visit relatives there, I cannot.

I listen to comments regularly from folks concerned about ethnic diversity who ask with a hint of guilt, "Why are no African-Americans or Latinos present or active in our organization?" It is another occasion when I simply do not know what to do and am tempted to show a photo of my mother, father and my fourteen siblings. In that photo, some of my brothers and sisters are darker than I am, some lighter; but there has never been a day in my life that I did not know I am black. My whole family knew we were black, and each of us was charged by our mother with proving by our exemplary behavior, intelligence and self-control that "Negroes are worthy of being integrated into the white community." It was never simply for my own acceptance that I twisted myself into a model of good behavior, but it was to demonstrate to whites that blacks are worthy of being loved and accepted as fully human beings.

So, I pushed on and pursued the best education I could find still hoping I could clear the hurdle that being black presented, that a good education would make a difference, and I would be accepted. How could anyone turn down a University of Chicago grad?

But on my way to graduation I was reminded that I was not home free yet.

The University of Chicago Divinity School required two years of academic work and then a year in residency with a local church. The Director of the Internship Program told me that my being engaged to marry a white woman made it impossible for him to arrange an internship for me, and I would have to search around for an opportunity of my own creation. Disappointed that another liberal institution had failed to provide the support I had every right to expect, I turned to friends I met during my undergraduate days at Oregon State University in Corvallis.

I had run out of money and was unable to return to Albion College for my junior year, and dropping out for a year and going to work to save some money seemed my only option. Tony Perrino, a student minister from Boston University who served my hometown church learned about my plan and insisted that I transfer to Oregon State and live with his family. Welcoming that option, I headed to Oregon, and friendships and connections made during that time enabled me to arrange an internship at the Wesley Foundation, First Methodist Church in Corvallis.

My fiancée had come along with me and went on to study at the University of Oregon in Eugene. It turned out that I was too far away for my own good, and she met and married another man. Not surprisingly, the traditional Oregon intrastate rivalry between the Ducks (U of Oregon) and the Beavers (Oregon State) takes on special intensity in my heart.

In addition, I discovered upon graduation in 1962 that Methodist Bishops did not appreciate the special challenge presented by the prospect of having to find a church appointment for an interracial couple. Bishop Charles Brashares in Chicago told me that interracial marriage was "the greatest possible disservice to the Christian cause," and there was "no way" I could be appointed to a church in the Chicago area. Later, the Open Housing Marches with Dr. King to Gage Park and other white neighborhoods of Chicago showed me just how right he probably was.

I wrote to all the most liberal bishops in the Methodist Church I could identify, and none would agree to accept me as a member of the Annual Conference, a geographic sector of churches over which they presided. All of them said in their own way that the appointment of an interracial couple was an impossibility. Bishop Kennedy of Southern California suggested I look for an appointment in Hawaii— which I did, with no luck.

Again, friends in Oregon prevailed. The Bishop there was persuaded that I could be a candidate for membership in the Oregon Conference and be placed "on trial", the standard probationary status of new applicants. My appointment to the campus ministry at Oregon State University was conditional upon my agreeing not to preach on the subject of race and not to date any *white* co-eds.

I scratch my head today wondering how I could have accepted those conditions. First and foremost, of course, the freedom to express the convictions you take to the pulpit should not be encumbered by anyone. That's not just my opinion but is expressed in the official documents of most denominations, including the Methodists.

White co-eds were the Bishop's other concern. Apparently, if I could have found co-eds of color, I could have dated them, but the only other blacks at Oregon State at that time were very large and quite ferocious football players. None of them appealed to me as an acceptable date.

One of those football players was invited by a student to a house dance at the residence of a white co-ed who was a member of the Wesley Foundation, the Methodist Student group at Oregon State. Her housemother threatened her with expulsion from the house if she did not cancel her date. She refused, so the housemother canceled the dance.

The coed brought her complaint to the Wesley Foundation, and her fellow students sent a letter in her support to the Oregon State *Barometer*. Several days after it was published, a cross was burned on the lawn of the First Methodist Church.

I decided it was time to re-think my commitment to integration at any cost and began to seek an appointment in Chicago where, years later, Harold Washington's mayoral campaign would seed the presidential bid of Barack Obama.

During the Obama campaign, critics in the black community raised questions about whether Obama was "black enough"—a complete U-turn in perception and expectations from the early days of integration when the only question was whether any candidate for elected office was white enough to win broad-based support—even among members of the black community. Jesse Jackson's presidential bids in 1984 and 1988 were limited to far fewer votes than Obama received because Jesse was very obviously "a really black candidate."

Jesse comes from the South and carries its cultural attributes proudly. He is a preacher, not a lawyer or scholar. His complexion, speaking style, uppity posture and his vocation as a preacher—one of the two professions (teachers and preachers) reserved for blacks leaders to serve their rightful role as keepers of the sheep. Jesse's style was supplemented by his activist role and his work as an organizer, prophet and agitator. Jesse was not one of the nation's beloved black preachers whose message usually made them proponents of racial peace at any price. For generations, blacks struggled to be respected by providing service as teachers and preachers. Even when volunteering to be soldiers, blacks found little to show that they were appreciated. The U.S. Army was segregated until a 1948 Executive Order from Harry Truman formally ended the practice. It could not, however, cure the underlying disease.

Consequently, seven of my nine brothers served in a segregated military. Five brothers served in World War II. Their comments about their experience were very guarded, but all of them were angry and hurt by seeing enemy prisoners given more courtesy and respect by white American soldiers than black soldiers ever received from those same GIs. Little wonder that rioting followed both World War I and World War II.

Although there was hardly ever any conversation about it, I was not alone among members of my family who suffered the pain of being black. Our stories offer some painful encounters with racism and racists along the road to freedom and equality—a destination several of us believed could only be reached by interracial marriage.

I am number ten of the fifteen children of Benjamin and Hazel Lawrence of Ballardvale, MA, and I have traveled a long and bumpy road from being "light, bright, damn near white" to being black and proud.

I owe an enormous debt of thanks to my parents
and to my siblings, for whom I thank God.

EPILOGUE

'WOKE UP THIS MORNING WITH MY MIND SET ON FREEDOM`

March 7, 2015 is a day that will live forever in the memory of every freedom-loving participant in the 50th re-enactment of the Selma to Montgomery March—especially those like me who had marched in Selma in 1965.

I knew the terror of being in a place where I was not wanted and where the opponents of voting rights for black Americans were uninhibited in demonstrating their First Amendment right to freely express their disdain for our cause and for our misguided choice of causes to support and folks to love.

Little wonder, then, that when the President of the United States stood at the foot of the Edmund Pettus Bridge to address us, my eyes began to water in an overpowering combination of pride and joy.

President Obama was introduced by John Lewis, a black U.S. Congressman who had been trampled by the Alabama State troopers in 1965. Today he was protected by those same troopers who proudly hosted additional security forces from Washington, Birmingham, and dozens of other communities to assure that John Lewis and our President were safe. John Lewis was introduced by the black, female Congressional representative, Terri Sewell, who now proudly represents the district that includes Selma.

President Obama stood on that infamous bridge and spoke with passion and power. Only President Lyndon B. Johnson before him with "... and we shall overcome" came close to having the courage Obama displayed for the cause of civil rights. There was a joy in the air that, for the first time in my life, made me giddy as I listened to my leader, the leader of the most powerful nation in the world. But there was something else: for once I had the joy of joining my president in sharing an overwhelming sense of being FREE!

President Obama has been battered and held hostage for so much of his presidency, but today our first black president and I, shared a newborn freedom!

To think that I had the good fortune to have marched over the Edmund Pettus Bridge in 1965, and today that bloodied bridge served as the platform for the President of the United States to finally find his freedom and deliver a personal Emancipation Proclamation to me.

There was nowhere for me to go and nowhere to turn to express the inner power of the connection between my contribution as one of thousands of freedom fighters who answered the call from Dr. King and the folks from Selma who fought and died for the right to vote. Combined with the triumph that the Obama Presidency carries, I just was not able to contain my joy, but I had the good sense to have asked my adult children to come along to Selma with me, and all four of them did. So, I fell into the arms of my older daughter who held me tight as tears of gratitude, joy and pride flowed freely from both of us.

And as if that was not enough.

After the Obama speech, we walked back toward the food tents, but I needed a rest for my 78 year-old bones and settled on the steps of the Selma Public Safety Building, when out of that building emerged the Rev. Jesse Jackson. Enjoying my new freedoms, I chased him and caught him and received for my trouble a bear hug and the warmest greeting imaginable: "Dick Lawrence, Dick Lawrence. This is my buddy. This is my buddy," Jesse shouted to anyone able to hear him. I just smiled and asked him if he would take a picture with the only one of my children present. He turned and greeted Valory with, "Yes, Yes. I met your babies at the hotel the other day." That he remembered them pleased us all and added an emotional exclamation mark to an incredible day.

Jesse had run for president in 1984 and 1988, and I was proud then to have been able to work some precincts for him in the New Hampshire primary.

Even though Jesse lost, I cannot help but feel his candidacy forced the nation to think seriously, for the first time, about the prospect of a black president. While there were way too many superstars and elected officials in Selma to provide him the attention he deserves, I cannot help but feel that his voice would have completed the chorus of speakers and preachers.

But my day was not over.

When I flew back into San Diego I was surprised that a TV reporter was waiting for me on the sidewalk at Lindberg Field. As the interview went on, I noticed that the Harbor Police Officer on traffic duty there was listening in, and he came up when I was finished and introduced himself. "Mr. Lawrence, I overheard you say that you were a Freedom Fighter and marched in Selma in 1965. I want you to know that before I was a police officer, I served as an officer in the military. People come up to me all the time and thank me for my service." After a brief pause and a quick brush of his hand over his eyes, he continued, "I just want you to know that I can only wish I would have had the courage you had to go to Selma, and I want to thank you for your service."

I could barely speak, but I thanked him and added, "We never know when a little extra effort will make a mark that makes more of a difference in the march toward freedom and justice than we could ever have imagined. I have been blessed and am deeply grateful for having lived a great life in a great period in our history."

A FINAL REFLECTION OR TWO

SAN DIEGO calls itself "America's Finest City" and may be the only place in the nation where the City Council could get away with declaring a State of Emergency "due to a severe shortage of affordable Housing," appoint a Task Force chaired by the former City Manager with the usual mix of interests fully represented, produce a long report with clear mandates of what must be done and then dissolve the State of Emergency after 15 years having done nothing to relieve the crisis. Nobody seemed to care.

I thought a State of Emergency was serious.

PHILANTHROPISTS AND FAMILY FOUNDATIONS SHOULD BE OUTLAWED unless the family foundation has a majority of the members on its Board of Trustees who are **not** family, and

Philanthropists do not put their name on the gifts they make.

It is astounding to me that the IRS lets families keep tax dollars in trust and then give them away to promote themselves: Ford, Rockefeller, Kellogg, Mellon, Gates, Jacobs, Cummins Engine Foundation, etc.

It is not uncommon to discover that some foundations created by families will hire a family member to run it, fill the Board with family members and pay them very generously to serve. Some have even concocted ways to provide scholarships exclusively to family members. (The IRS frowns on that practice now.)

My boss at Cummins Engine Foundation, Irwin Miller, made a clear distinction between charity and self-promotion. He held that any gift from which his company benefits in any way is NOT philanthropy at all. It is a tax-exempt company contribution.

I wish we all treated every foundation as responsible to us, the taxpayers, because foundations are using funds that would otherwise be in the public till. Not that the government does a great job with our tax dollars, but at least the government does not act as if they are God's angels capable of only doing good for us.

RESURRECTION is usually thought to be a special gift God provided for Jesus,

I do not think so.

This year, with the election of Trump, I fell into a wormhole. I could not escape the feeling that all the work of the Freedom Movements had been for naught and my personal commitment to them had been buried in an era of the wealthy not only corralling 99% of the money but also taking control of the most powerful nation on earth..

But as the Easter Season approached, I found myself energized, alert, creative and willing once again to take on anything the times had to dish out. I call that resurgence my personal resurrection.

I cannot explain this phenomenon, but I doubt that my personal resurrection is exclusive.

Am I right?

NOW, ABOUT THOSE METHODISTS

God never intended for there to be any black Methodists.

It is not well known, but the Methodist Church split over the issue of slavery, and for years there were two churches—Methodists north and Methodists south.

In an effort to UNIFY the church, the Methodists created a separate jurisdiction into which all black churches and black preachers were assigned. It was called quite curiously, the Central Jurisdiction.

Growing up in a little town in Massachusetts, I knew nothing of this history or church structure. So, when a young seminarian from the Boston University School of Theology came to Ballardvale and re-opened the small Methodist Church there, I was unknowingly given a chance to make history.

Having been active in the Ballardvale Congregational Church where I went to Sunday

School and sang in the youth choir, I faced my first major theological question: was I destined to be a Methodist or a Congregationalist?

Pondering this academic question as occupants of an Ivory Tower usually do, meant I had plenty of time to make a decision. Then the BU Seminarian organized a Youth Baseball Team.

The question suddenly became more compelling: was I destined to sing in the Congregational Church Choir or play catcher on the Methodist Church Baseball Team?

Blame the Red Sox if you want. I wanted to play for them and help them beat the Yankees and win a pennant—maybe even a World Series, so I joined the Methodist Church baseball team (and the church). That BU Seminarian would not relent and later steered me to the Methodist Ministry.

That's where the REAL TROUBLE started.

There were not enough Negroes in New England where I earned my Local Preacher's License for the "colored" Central Jurisdiction to exist, so I was automatically a member of the white Methodist structure.

When I finally decided to pursue a graduate degree in theology, I did not go to a seminary. I went to the University of Chicago Divinity school which operated at that time with a Federated Theological Faculty that included the Baptist, Congregational, Unitarian and Disciples of Christ graduate schools of theology. Failing to enroll in a Methodist seminary made me a suspicious candidate for ministry in the Methodists eyes, but I was accepted as a candidate for ministry in the Oregon Conference after serving a year-long residency at the First Methodist Church in Corvallis with the chaplain to Methodist students at Oregon State University. The first step into full membership for everyone is usually two years "on trial."

Even to gain "on trial" status and an appointment to a local church from the Oregon Bishop, I had to agree that I would not preach on the subject of race nor would I date any white coeds.

I kept my promise, but I discovered an old girl friend had graduated and was still single, and we began a courtship that resulted in an interracial marriage.

I had been told previously by the Bishop in Chicago that an interracial marriage "would be the greatest possible disservice to the cause of race relations." So it was no surprise that I could not get an appointment in the Oregon Conference without the active lobbying and support from respected pastors in the Conference.

The local church in Corvallis surprised me with broad support for our wedding, but that ended when our first child arrived about three months too early—a possibility I had not discussed with any of the church officials.

The Board of Ministry found at the annual assessment for ministry that my engaging in pre-marital sex provided serious reasons to question my qualifications for ministry. However, to defrock me was too harsh, I would guess, because too many of the members of the Board of Ministry most likely had pre-marital sex themselves, so they extended my time "on trial." But the Bishop refused to appoint me. We moved back to Chicago, and I applied for membership in the Northern Illinois Conference (Chicago Area). The Bishop there refused.

Pressure was once again organized and applied on the church leader, and the Bishop relented provided my wife and I would agree to go for a psychological evaluation. We said NO. My wife was not a candidate for ministry, but I did agree to see a psychiatrist of their choosing. He completed his assessment and sent a letter attesting to my mental health and added, "The only question that remains in my mind is why would such an intelligent person as Mr. Lawrence want to be a Methodist minister."

I was admitted "on trial."

And it still goes on today in 2017.

The Methodist Church is huge—the third largest denomination in the U.S. They elect bishops, and one of them is a lesbian named Karen Oliveto. Church law bars clergy who are "self-avowed practicing homosexuals," so the church's Judicial Council met, deliberated and decreed that a decision must be made about whether Bishop Oliveto can remain in her position. They just didn't make that decision—partly because not only is Bishop Oliveto in violation of church law, so are the bishops who participated in her consecration.

Oliveto was elected last year by members of the Western Jurisdiction of the Church, and immediately after, her election was challenged by members of the South Central Jurisdiction (Oklahoma).

A special national conference of church members will be convened in 2019 to decide her fate, and the fate of those who consecrated her.

Of special concern is the development of a fracture group of Evangelical Methodists who insist that church policy be enforced and LGBT clergy be defrocked.

Clearly there are those on the other side of the issue who are fighting to lift prohibitions on gay clergy.

THE CIVIL RIGHTS MOVEMENT was called the second revolutionary movement in the United States by Condoleezza Rice. She earlier said, "The United States was born with a birth defect."

TRIBUTE TO THE REV.
DR. MARTIN LUTHER KING JR.

United African American Ministerial Action Council Community Breakfast Celebration, Jan. 18, 2016

THE LEGACY OF THE REV. DR. MARTIN LUTHER KING, JR., A SPEECH BY THE REV. RICHARD LAWRENCE

INTRODUCTION

Albion College, my alma mater, is located in a small town in Michigan (Albion), and I was invited to spend the 1956 Thanksgiving holiday break with my college roommate in his home in the Detroit suburb of Royal Oak. (The name, Royal Oak, sounds like they had only one tree—but I'm sure it is a ROYAL one.)

When we arrived, my roommate's father came hurriedly down the stairs to greet us with the news that he was late because "he just had to finish a great book which proved beyond a shadow of a doubt that gorillas are superior to Negroes."

I stood dumbfounded and silent, and so did my roommate who then proceeded to introduce me to his dad whose hand I shook without saying a word.

How come? Why was I silent?

Because I had not met Dr. King yet, and

Because I had not yet lived through the era of black power, black consciousness and black pride and did not know that I was black and beautiful and proud and had no reason to keep quiet about being who I am.

I grew up in all-white community in Massachusetts (Ballardvale—part of Andover). Because my mother was a very light complexioned African-American, and my father was very dark, we ran the gamut of shades of black among the 15 children they produced.

I learned how to survive in the white community, and I learned how to survive in the black community and am really very much at ease in both. However, I am not at home in either.

I had invested so much when I was younger in being accepted by whites that I rarely said a word no matter how badly I was treated. I took the pain and kept it to myself.

But along came the civil rights movement, and after Dr. King's assassination, the black power, black consciousness, black nationalism movement, and I learned to stand up for who I am and what I believe.

I hope to convince you that we dare not sit in a room where we propose to honor Dr. King unless we are ready to face the challenge of Dr. King's commitment to stand up for non-violence and economic justice.

LET ME TAKE ON THE EASY ONE FIRST: ECONOMIC JUSTICE

I have not forgotten occupy… nor have I forgotten labor strikes like the bread and roses strike in the textile mills of Lawrence, MA and the boycotts of grapes and lettuce to support Cesar Chavez and the Farm Workers Union. I have not forgotten our ongoing battles here in San Diego to establish a living wage and health care benefits for all workers and balance the profits of doing business with a commitment to community benefits with doing good—like JMI Realty played a courageous role by striking a legally binding community benefits agreement with ACCORD (A Community Coalition Organized For Responsible Development).—Pause –

I am so glad Bernie Sanders is running for president... and that he might win.... The more successful his campaign, the more likely we might finally have a serious, national debate about how well our economy is doing on the scale that measures economic justice vs unrelenting profits and greed.

Nobody can convince me that having 1% of the population controlling 99% of this country's wealth is the best a capitalistic country committed to democracy can do or that we can bail out banks but cannot house and care for homeless families and veterans. That we will focus so much on profits that we will threaten the life of the planet that supports us.

The base rung on the ladder of justice is distributive justice which is easy to identify when you see it— or when you don't. Distributive justice would feature a reasonable sample of all groups—age, race, gender, etc. At all levels of a business or organization.

The best example of organizing around distributive justice was Dr. King's Southern Christian Leadership Conference's Operation Breadbasket in Chicago. It was a minister's steering committee organized to assess how fairly the companies doing business in the black community were doing with hiring and the use of black suppliers and contractors. If a company failed to meet the standard, Breadbasket would boycott the business until a covenant was signed that committed the company to employment and business goals for blacks.

Restorative Justice—is the level where we recognize the failures of the past and act to correct those deficits. The Marshall Plan and the early days of reconstruction and later affirmative action were acts of restorative justice.

Creative Justice—is the unqualified attempt to do what must be done to contribute to the fullest possible development of every human being. It is called simply love.

Dr. King echoes the call of the prophet Micah:

Do justice. Love mercy (kindness). Walk humbly with your god.

OKAY, THAT WAS EASY, RIGHT? SO LET'S TACKLE THE TOUGH ONE: NON-VIOLENCE

We like to think today that Dr. King was loved and supported by everyone... that we were all in for him. But the marches with him in Chicago caused Dr. King to say:

> *"I've been in demonstrations all across the South, but I can say that I have never seen...mobs as hostile and hate-filled as I've seen in Chicago."*

I'd like to suggest that his assassination ought to cast a final and fairly heavy cloud over the thought that he was universally loved.

Dr. King struggled with the question of police power/police forces—local and national.

Remember, Sheriff Clark? He was the local policing force in Selma and had a message for those of us who were headed to Selma in 1965 for the march to Montgomery:

"It is not my job, he said, to protect 'outsiders who come to Alabama to make trouble,' so if you're coming to Selma, you are on your own."

Dr. King implores us to dig deep and think long about violence and non-violence which we experience today primarily with our local police and the use of deadly force.

We have a problem with our police forces across the land. No more than sheriffs in the south had a right to beat peaceful demonstrators because the community they believed they were serving thought demonstrators to be less than human, do police officers today have the right to dispense with troublemakers in any way they choose. Police officers retain and restrain so the court can deliberate and make a thoughtful judgment and deliver punishment if the offender is found guilty.

Death sentences nor any other punishment should be delivered on the streets at the hands of arresting officers. "Black lives matter" is a reminder to us that all lives matter.

And if we go back and look at the issue of justice and discover that for some reason the number of people killed on the street represent a disproportionate number of blacks or youth or hippies or gays or women... we need to do justice. We need to find a cure for whatever or from wherever that injustice originates.

Police officers and citizens alike need to make a commitment to non-violence.

We also have a problem with our military policing power and face the fact that we cannot bomb away the enemies we face today.

Our enemy today sneaks up on us... on unsuspecting victims across the globe and shoots workers in San Bernardino or bombs or guns down uninvolved people in cafes in France or crashes airplanes into workers in the World Trade Center towers in NYC.

I am ashamed when one of those terrorists bombers is an American, and I cannot help but think that somehow the central message there is that we have failed... that I have failed. That an injustice has been done that we need to fix.

CONCLUSION

Malcolm X and Dr. King debated philosophies of social change like Booker T. Washington and W.E.B.

Dubois did, and at the heart of the matter was the issue of love and power.

Dr. King finally clarified for me the relationship between the two when he said. "We have to get this right: power without love is reckless and abusive. Love without power is sentimental and anemic."

Love—Power—Justice.

Many of you deserve to be up here. Odetta is singing at the other MLK celebration this morning and as I have been designated her driver, I know she is going to lead the crowd in singing "This Little Light Of Mine."

Will you join me in ending our reflections on the life and work of Dr. King by looking around and going to folks you see here today who have worked for economic justice and non-violence? Call out their names and reach out to them: "Thank you for your service."

March proudly if your name is called so we might all appreciate how many of us there are who are working to celebrate Dr. King's challenge to overpower chaos by creating a community built on economic justice and non-violence.

If no one calls your name and you want to stand up and march toward the beloved community, come on by and let me shake your hand and thank you for your service.

Amen.

I can get us going as I look over the audience and see: Jamie Gates, Sue Reynolds, Cory Briggs, John Kratzer,

Herb Shore, Virginia Franco, Wendell French, Lee Van Ham, Victor Bloomberg, Pedro Quiroz, Theresa Quiroz, Gregg Robinson, Richard Barera, Robbie Robinson, Gerald Brown, Lori Causky, Bishop Kokayi, Bishop McKinney, Bishop Dixon, Gloria Cooper, Pastor Dempsy, Pastor Hill, Mark Jones, Aaron Henry, Pastor Terrell Fletcher, Kent Peters, Norma Chavez Peterson, Clare Crawford, Mickey Kasparian, Ken Grimes.

That's how I think we celebrate and keep alive the memory and the message of the Rev. Dr. Martin Luther King, Jr.: by standing tall and marching to protect our freedom.

Stand with me now to show each other that there are enough of us in this room to set the record straight.

Thank you. Thank you. Thank you

Amen. Amen. Amen.

"What we need is a new Bottom Line, one which judges the various aspects of society by the qualities they cultivate in us... we [should] expect our society to promote love... compassion, kindness and generosity, ...ethical and ecological sensitivity... [and we should] expect our society to nurture our capacity to respond to others as embodiments of the sacred and to the universe with gratitude, wonder and awe." –Rabbi Michael Lerner

A VERY SPECIAL PRESENT FOR MY 70TH BIRTHDAY
FROM THE SAN DIEGO CITY COUNCIL

Resolution Of The City Council
City Of San Diego

RICHARD LAWRENCE DAY

Presented by Councilmember Toni Atkins

WHEREAS, Richard Lawrence will celebrate his 70th birthday and an extraordinary life of service in community development and social justice on Friday, November 10th, 2006; and

WHEREAS, Richard Lawrence is a true community hero, an ordained Methodist minister and a veteran of the Civil Rights Movement who brushed shoulders with the great social justice giants of our era; and

WHEREAS, Richard Lawrence stood with the Rev. Dr. Martin Luther King, Jr. in protest of lending and hiring practices that discriminated against African Americans; and drove an old VW bus down to the Selma, Alabama with food for civil rights demonstrators and joined the Selma to Montgomery March for voting rights; and worked with the Rev. Jesse Jackson's Rainbow Coalition and Operation PUSH; and

WHEREAS, as a two-term City Council Member in Lawrence, MA, **Richard Lawrence** led efforts to revitalize a former textile manufacturing town suffering from poverty and neglect, served as chair of the city's Charter Review Committee and the Small Business Revolving Loan Fund, and as vice-chair of the Housing and Economic Development Committee; and

WHEREAS, Richard Lawrence also directed the start-up of the Greater Lawrence Community Foundation, and spent nearly 15 years with Cummins Engine, working in management, plant operations, personnel, and as the program director of minority community development programs for the Cummins Engine Foundation; and

WHEREAS, Richard Lawrence's San Diego legacy includes work on the 45-acre City of Villages project in Southeastern San Diego, which when completed will bring to the area new commercial and retail businesses, more than 800 affordable housing units, and several hundred jobs; and

WHEREAS, Richard Lawrence is so known and beloved by housing advocates throughout San Diego that he was named the Housing Federation's Advocate of the Year for his work with the Affordable Housing Coalition and the City of San Diego's Affordable Housing Task Force; and

WHEREAS, Richard Lawrence has also shared his wealth of experience and knowledge as a member of the boards of the Independent Gaming Review Board (Viejas Band of Kumeyaay Indians), Children Having Children/Project New Village, Interfaith Committee for Worker Justice, A Community Coalition Organized for Responsible Development(ACCORD), Center for Policy Initiatives (CPI), Interreligious Foundation for Community Organization (IFCO), National Black United Fund, Consumer Appeals Board – Ford Motor Company, NAACP Executive Board of Merrimack Valley, MA, Habitat for Humanity in Lawrence, MA, International Institute of Greater Lawrence, and YMCA of Greater Lawrence; and

WHEREAS, extending his labor of love, **Richard Lawrence** has also served as a Commissioner of the Lawrence Human Rights Commission, Chair of Black Methodists for Church Renewal and the Negotiations Committee of Operation Breadbasket in Chicago, and as a founding member of the Association of Black Foundation Executives; and

WHEREAS, as an inspiration to his four talented children, Valory, Abigail, Tony, and Benjamin, **Richard Lawrence** finds time to renew himself through music, golf, camping with his wife, Nancy, catching Joan Baez concerts, and playing with his cherished grandchildren, Anthony, Isabella, and Richie; and therefore **BE IT RESOLVED,** by the Mayor and Council of the City of San Diego, that this Council, for and on behalf of the people of San Diego, does hereby recognize **Richard Lawrence** for a lifelong commitment to a ministry of interracial and economic justice, and join with his friends and family in wishing Richard joy and laughter on his 70th birthday; and **BE IT FURTHER RESOLVED,** that Friday, November 10, 2006 is hereby proclaimed to be **"RICHARD LAWRENCE DAY"** in the City of San Diego. (Prepared by Toni Atkins with help from Richard's kids.)